画报出版社

舊中國掠影

旧中国掠影

　　历史的巨轮轰然辗过公元一千九百四十九年,中国以一副崭新的容貌崛起在世界东方。由此上溯到1912年,推翻帝制,成立中华民国;直至1840年,中英鸦片战争爆发,封建王朝锁国的大门被西方列强的坚船利炮叩开—我们将这一个多世纪的中国称为半封建半殖民地的中国;相对社会主义新中国而言,我们又概括称之为"旧中国"。

　　回顾旧中国走过的艰难痛苦的历程,心情格外沉重,浮现在我们眼前的是政治上愈演愈烈的腐败,排斥异己、军阀混战;经济上极为缓慢的增长,绝大多数中国人在仅能活命的生活水平线上下挣扎;外交上一次又一次的丧权辱国、割地赔款,美丽富饶的中华大地被宰割得七零八落。一次又一次的挫折,一次又一次的失败……

　　然而,历史的曙光终将冲破黎明前的黑暗,几千年的文明古国终将卸下不堪承载的重负,新中国的康庄大道必将取代旧中国泥泞的死胡同;如今,十亿炎黄子孙正沿着这条康庄大道,以前所未有的速度,向着光辉灿烂的二十一世纪飞奔。

　　忘记历史就意味着背叛!不了解历史就无法对我们今天身处的这个时代有清醒的认识,也会因为辨别不清前途而再度陷入泥潭。看不到旧中国政治的腐败,就体会不到新中国制度的优越;看不到旧中国经济增长的缓慢,就体会不到新中国经济的腾飞;看不到旧中国外交上的丧权辱国,就体会不到作为当代中国人的自豪……

　　了解历史有多种途径,我们一般是通过以文字方式记载的史籍。史籍固然较为全面,但它亦有致命的弱点——不够直观。随着科学技术的发展,照相机这一绝妙的发明把人类带入了通过图像直观地管窥历史的新纪元。中国自从1844年诞生了第一张照片,从此,形形色色的人摄下了五花八门的照片,为我们留下了一大笔异常珍贵的遗产。今天,我们正是利用这笔遗产,从几千幅前人留下的照片中精选八百余幅,加以分门别类,编辑成这部影集,奉献给亲爱的读者朋友。

　　本部影集的内容极为广泛,包括旧中国的上层政治、刀光剑影中的军事活动、蒙耻遭辱的外交活动、国计民生的经济贸易、异彩纷呈的各类民族服饰、恭敬虔诚的宗教迷信、以及城市风光、人文景观、交通状况、天灾赈济、文教卫生,还有形形色色的人物众生相。我们试图通过上述丰富、翔实的图片,将旧中国方方面面的瞬间呈现出来,再借助您的想象,将这近千个瞬间拼接、揉和,联成流动的画面,从而使您一览旧中国全景。

　　本部影集在内容上还有一大特色:为了不与已出版的诸如中国近代史、现代史、中国革命史,以及各种专题影集,如中国人民解放军战史、辛亥革命、抗日战争等诸多题材的影集重复,我们对这类题材的图片一律忍痛割爱,这从另一个角度来讲,也正好符合我们编辑本影集反映旧中国的主导思想。

　　本部影集所收照片时空跨度极大,从空间角度来看,北起白山黑水,南至天涯海角,西起黄土高原,东至大海台岛,几乎遍及整个中华大地,内容上基本达到了我们照顾全国各地、各民族,使之大致平衡的初衷;可惜的是旧中国的西南、西北内地、少数民族聚居地非常封闭,人迹罕至,所以可供选择的资料过少。从时间角度来看,下限时间当然是1949年,上限时间直达1869年,前后跨越八十年。为了使全集的内容相对集中与紧凑,形成照片内容及线索的联系,我们又把重点放在1900年至1949年之间。

　　为了使读者朋友明确每幅照片所反映的特定内容,我们对每一张入选照片的有关资料无不进行了极为细致、繁琐的考证,尽可能详细地标明地区、民族、人物、背景等情况,还注明了照片拍摄的年代。凡经多方考证,一时尚难以判定准确年代的,我们采用一些相对准确的时间概念标明,比如"清末"(指1900年前后至1911年);"民初"(指1912年至1927年);"民国"(指1928年至1937年);"抗战"(或称"日伪",指1937年至1945年);"抗战后"(指1945年至1949年);等等。

　　另外需要指出的是:这些反映旧中国历史风貌的照片,大部分出自我们通常所说的"反面人物"之手,此外还有部分出自洋人的炫耀或猎奇之心、"慈善家"的"关怀"之意,等等。每按动一次快门,无疑就记录下了一个客观存在的瞬间,但是,每幅照片都是拍摄者经过素材选择、拍摄立意、拍摄角度等潜心设计之后的"作品",它又肯定打上了作者主观意向的烙印,或真实、或奉承、或宣传、或掠夺;这就需要读者朋友从主客观两个方面入手,去分析解剖这些照片,从而得出正确的认识和公正的评论。

　　亲爱的读者,当我们编完这部影集,心里实在留下太多的遗憾—资料和版面的双重限制,使我们不得不舍弃了许多无论照片内容还是照片质量均属上乘的历史镜头。保留下来的这有限的八百余幅照片,对于一百多年旧中国的风风雨雨来讲,实在微乎其微,充其量也只能算作旧中国的"掠影",所以我们将影集的名称定为"旧中国掠影"。但是,常言说得好,"百闻不如一见",我们坚信,这部影集会带您步入真实的旧中国。您也许会怒其不争,也许会痛斥妖魔,也许会沉思历史,也许会扼腕长叹……。但最终您将深受启迪,心灵深处真情涌动,为中华民族更加繁荣富强的明天,去进取,去奋斗。

A GLIMPSE OF OLD CHINA

The year 1949. China stands in the world with a totally new look. The year 1912. China's last emperor was deposed with the founding of Republic of China. The year 1840. The gate of feudal China was opened by the rumble of gunfire in the Sino-British Opium War, turning the country into a semicolonial and semifeudal society which lasted for more than a century. This period is referred to as "Old China" compared with the socialist New China.

Heavy is the heart whenever looking back to this period of history: the corrupted rulers, the endless wars, the slowly developed economy, the people in deep distress, and, the foreign policies humiliating the country and forfeiting its sovereignty....

However, the dawn of history eventually broke the darkness. The Chinese civilization of thousands of years unloaded the heavy burden with the founding of New China. Today, all the children of the Yellow Emperor are on the way to prosperity and striving forward towards the 21st century.

Nothing is more betrayal than forgetting the past. One can never clearly define today unless he knows quite well about history. He would never see the superiority of New China without comparing with the corrupted politics in Old China. Nobody knows how fast that economy has developed since 1949 if he has no idea of how slow it was in Old China. No one will be proud of being a Chinese unless he knows how humiliating of being a Chinese caused by foreign policies in Old China....

There are many ways of knowing history. The most common one is through historical records in written form. Although completely recording all walks of life in the past, books are not ocular enough to record history. Cameras, a fantastic invention of the human beings, make it easier to perceive history directly through the senses. Since the birth of the first photo in 1844 in China, a great number of precious heritage have been left behind in pictures. Now we are lucky enough to make good use of these pictures and select 800 out of thousands of them with great care. Here we present this picture album to our readers.

Our picture album contains almost all aspects in Old China. They include royal politics, military and foreign affairs, national economy and trade, national costumes, religion and urban sightseeings, in addition to landscapes, communications, natural disaster relief, culture, education and public health, as well as various figures. We try to depict a full picture of Old China through these photos.

To get rid of repeating the same topics with many picture albums specializing in modern and contemporary Chinese history, the Chinese revolutionary history, the PLA war history, the Revolution of 1911 and the Resistant War Against Japan, we part reluctantly with what we treasure and follow the main theme of this picture album.

The photos we select here have a large span in time and space: the snow-capped mountains and black rivers in the north, the end of the earth in the south, the Yellow Loess Plateau in the west and the vast seas and islands in the east. Nevertheless, it is a pity that we have limited choice from materials left behind to display life in southwestern and northwestern Old China densely populated with minority people because it was very closed in these areas at that time; Time spans from 1869 to 1949, which we lay stress on the peirod through 1990 and 1949.

We have endeavored great effort in examining and proving all related materials for each photo we select so as to provide our readers with precise information, such as place, monority, figure and backgroung, and, time that the picture was taken. For those hard to make for sure, we use some standard terms for time, such as the late Qing Dynasty (1900-1911), the early Republic of China (1912-1927), Republic of China (1928-1937), the Resistant War Against Japan (or *riwei*, 1937-1945), the posterior RWAJ (1945-1949), etc.

One more we want to declear is that the majority of these pictures are collected from those we usually called "nagative characters." Some of them are from foreigners. Each time when photographer clickes the shutter records the snapshot of the objective existence. However, each picture is a work that the photographer designs with great care. It is a brand of the photographer's subjective purpose, maybe true, flattering, propaganda or plundering. We believe that our readers can get their own idea.

Dear readers, when completing compiling this picture album, we still feel sorry to give up numerous fine-quality pictures because of the limitation of material and space of the page. It is far from enough to depict Old China lasting for more than a century with some 800 pictures, which can only lead you to have a glimpse of the era. That's why we entitle the picture album *A Glimpse of Old China*. As an old saying goes, seeing is believing. We do hope that this picture album can bring you back to the time it belongs. No matter what kind of feeling it brings about, you will be enlightened and become more confident for the future of New China!

政治篇

POLITICS

回顾旧中国的政治,犹如步入一个风雨飘摇的漫漫长夜。短短百年之间,偌大个中国经历了一次又一次的阵痛:最后一个封建王朝满清政府的衰亡、中华民国的建立、伪满洲国及伪国民政府的建立与消灭.直至1949年中华民国在大陆的统治被推翻,中华人民共和国成立,才彻底宣告了旧中国政治的结束。

沿着以上这条旧中国政治的发展脉络,本篇精选了百余幅珍贵的历史照片,它们大致又可分为如下三个部分:

晚清政治:包括1900年八国联军侵华战争之后《辛丑条约》的签订、清末的立宪活动、西太后及光绪皇帝的"驾崩"、宣统的继位与退位等重大政治活动和事件。

民国初期政治:包括民国临时政府的建立、袁世凯及北洋政府的统治、各政党的建立和国会议员的选举、洪宪帝制、庆祝第一次世界大战协约国胜利、国民会议,等等。

日本侵华战争时期敌占区的政治:包括"七·七事变"前日本在满洲、华北的政治活动、侵华战争爆发后南京伪维新政府、华北伪政府的建立,以及伪国民政府、伪华北政务委员会的成立,还有这一时期华北伪政府与日本、伪满洲国相互勾结,推行"华北治安强化运动"、成立伪新民会,等等。

这组照片中有许多是首次公开发表,展现了旧中国一些鲜为人知的重要政治活动、事件的场面。

需要说明的是,1945年至1949年的照片,因广为人知,故我们在此极少收录。

The politics of Old China seems to be covered by an endless darkness. In a period of only one hundred years, the once-mighty Middle Kingdom experienced one loss after another: the collapse of the last feudal dynasty, the establishment of the Republic of China, the Japanese control of Manchuria, and finally the establishment of the nationalist government and its demise. The old political system did not come to an end until the found of the People's Republic of China in 1949.

According to the chronological order, this chapter arranges a hundred or so rare historical photographs in three parts: the later years of the Qing Dynasty, the early days of the Republic of China, and the Sino-Japanese War Period.

Many of the photographs in this chapter, which reveal some of the former secret political activities and incidents, are being published for the first time. Pictures between 1945 and 1949 in this chapter are few because of their wide publication.

Yi Kuang and Li Hongzhang, plenipoten- 　1901年9月7日，清朝全权大臣奕劻
tiary representatives of the Qing 李鸿章与英美法俄等十一国公使
government, signed the Peace Treaty of 订立《辛丑条约》。图为条约签订
1901 with eleven countries on Sept. 7, 时各国公使的合影。
1901, in the wake of the Boxer Uprising.

In August 1900 the siege of Beijing was broken by an international expeditionary force that included American, British, French, German, Russian and Japanese troops. This picture shows the allied forces slaughtering the Boxers.

1900年英美法俄等国组成"八国联军",发动大规模侵华战争。图系"八国联军"攻入北京城后,在齐化门外屠杀义和团的情景。

On June 2, 1900, the German envoy Ketteler Klemens, on his way to the Ministry of Foreign Affairs, fell into conflict with the Prince of Duan and was killed by his soldiers at Dongdanpailou, Beijing. That became known as the Ketteler Incident. On January 18, 1903, an arch in honor of the German envoy was completed at the entrance to Dongdan Street. Manchu officials and representatives of the allied forces attended the completion ceremony. This photo shows Zai Feng, the Prince of Chun, offering a sacrifice.

1900年6月2日德国公使克林德乘轿车前往总理衙门会晤,途经东单牌楼,与清军发生冲突,被端王载漪的虎神营士兵开枪打死,遂酿成克林德事件。1903年1月18日,清朝官员及"八国联军"在东单路口,举行为德国公使克林德修建的牌坊建成典礼。图为清朝政府命醇贤亲王载沣前往致祭时的照片。

Empress Dowager Cixi died on November 15, 1908. Here is a section of her funeral procession.

1908年11月15日慈禧太后去世。这是举行慈禧奉安大典的仪仗队伍一瞥。

On January 3, 1902, Empress Dowager Cixi went from Zhengding (present Shijiazhuang, Hebei), to Baoding by train and arrived at Majiabao Railway Station, Beijing, four days later. Then, she, in a sedan chair, returned to her palace from Zhengyangmen, which she had fled during the allied forces' invasion. The picture above shows Shan Qi, the Prince of Su, meeting the Empress Dowager.

1902年1月3日，慈禧太后自直隶正定(今河北省石家庄)乘火车至保定，7日自保定至北京马家堡车站，而后乘肩舆从永定门入正阳门还宫。此系肃亲王善耆等迎接慈禧太后回銮的情景。

Emperor Guanyxu died on November 14, 1908. In December, his coffin was moved from Huangshoudian to Guandedian (in present Jingshan Park). His funeral was held in May 1910.

1908年11月14日清德宗光绪帝载恬去世。同年12月光绪梓宫由寿皇殿移至景山观德殿。1910年5月又移至梁各庄暂安。图为1910年5月光绪奉安大典移梓宫于梁各庄时沿途设立的第一站薰殿。

Zai Tao (front, on horse back), a prince of the Qing Dynasty, inspecting the government-run Luanzhou Mine in 1911.

1911年清朝王爷、禁卫军大臣载涛视察北洋滦州官矿有限公司，下榻于该公司。前面骑马者为载涛。

In 1913, the abdicated Empress Dowager Longyu died. The republican government and the former royal family held a grand funeral for her. Longyu (1868 — 1913), was the niece of Cixi, and the wife of Emperor Guangxu. In 1909, she was venerated empress dowager and administrated state affairs as a regent. Three years later, she declared the abdication of the Qing Dynasty.

1913年，主持清帝逊位的隆裕太后病死，袁世凯政府及清皇室为隆裕太后举行大规模的公祭和丧葬仪式。此系太和门公祭活动情形。隆裕太后 (1868—1913)，满洲镶黄旗人，叶赫那拉氏，系慈禧太后的侄女，为光绪皇后，1909年尊为皇太后垂帘听政。1912年被迫宣布清帝退位。

Dr. Sun Yet-sen handed over his presidency to Yuan Shikai in April 1912. This group photograph was taken when his cabinet members were giving a send-off to Dr. Sun. Front row, the middle three, left to right are Liang Shiyi, Sun Yet-sen and Huang Xing.

1912年4月孙中山宣布解除中华民国临时大总统之职，让位于袁世凯。图为孙中山宣布解职后，原内阁成员欢送孙中山时的合影。前排左起第二人为梁士诒，第三人为孙中山，第四人为黄兴。

On the first anniversary of the 1911 Republican Revolution, which lead to the overthrow of the Manchu Dynasty, martyrs of the revolution were honored.

1912年10月10日北京辛亥革命纪念会设立的"中华民国为国死事诸君灵台"。

In 1912, Liang Qichao, Tang Hualong and Lin Changmin organized the Democratic Party in an attempt to form a third party in opposition to the existing Republican Party, which was manipulated by Yuan Shikai, and Kuomintang. Liang Qichao was elected leader of the Democratic Party. Here is a group photograph of the party members.

1912年梁启超、汤化龙、林长民等组成民主党，推举梁启超为该党领袖，试图成为临时国会中与袁世凯操纵的共和党、孙中山等领导的国民党抗衡的第三大党。这是该党成立后召开本部临时大会时的合影。

Democratic Party members at Beijing University, October 1912.

1912年10月北京大学民主党党员合影

An official banquet during the Qing Dynasty.

清代官员的公宴

The Kyakhta Negotiation, between China and Russia, led to the signature of the *Treaty of China, Russia and Mongolia* on June 7, 1915. Here is a group photo of Chinese and Russian representatives attending the negotiation.

1915年6月7日中俄恰克图会议签订《中俄蒙协约》时，中方代表陈箓等与俄方代表的合影。

Yuan Shikai, as emperor, in his newly designed military dress.

袁世凯身着新设计的洪宪皇帝戎装。

China Moslem Promotion Society, the first of its kind in China, was founded in 1912 with the headquarters in Beijing. In 1915, the society became a part of the citizen petition corps, which was organized by Yuan Shikai in an attempt to proclaim himself emperor. Here is a group photo of the society taken on December 13, 1915, the same day Yuan Shikai ascended the throne.

1912年，"中国回教俱进会"成立，这是近代中国第一个统一的穆斯林组织，总部设在北京。1915年袁世凯为复辟帝制，操纵所谓公民请愿团，为变更国体制造舆论。"中国回教俱进会"本部、全国回教回族公民联合请愿团全体代表暨职员，在1915年12月13日袁世凯宣布称帝"解决国体"问题后合影留念。

In an attempt to legitimize himself as emperor, Yuan Shikai led government officials to offer sacrifices at the Temple of Heaven on December 23, 1914. Such sacrifices were only conducted by emperors prior to the overthrow of the Qing Dynasty.

1914年12月23日袁世凯为复辟帝制，率文武百官到天坛"祀天"，此系祭天仪式之一——宣读祭文。

In 1920, the Beiyang government sent the special envoy Xu Shuzheng to recognize Jebtsun Damba, Living Buddha of Outer Mongolia. Here is a group photograph of Xu Shuzheng (standing in the middle with a black arm band) and Outer Mongolian high-ranking officials in front of the Monastery of Erdeni Dzu.

1920年北洋政府册封外蒙活佛哲布尊丹巴,此为特派专使徐树铮(前排中立臂带黑圈者)在库伦大庙前与其随员及外蒙上层人士合影。

The capital police office destroying opium for the third time on February 3, 1921.

1921年2月3日,京师军警督察处第三次焚毁烟土。

In 1928, Libaji in the east of Henan Province was acknowledged as a county ruled by "Minquan", which was derived from Dr. Sun Yet-sen's Three Principles of the People — Minzu (Nationalism), Minquan (Democracy) and Minsheng (livelihood). Here are officials of the new county.

1928年在河南省东部李坝集设县,取名"民权",源自孙中山先生三民主义中的"民权"。图为民权县开办时官员纪念合影。

Former officials of the Qing Dynasty during the republican period. Left to right: Bao Xi, Zhang Quan, Fu Kaisen, Fu Tong, Feng Shu, Zhu Chen, (?), Li Yuying.

民国时期在北京的清朝遗老合影。左起宝熙、张权、福开森、溥桐、冯恕、朱琛、×××、李煜瀛。

On Oct. 5, 1923, Cao Kun was elected president by the national congress. Five days later he took the office. Here is a group photograph of the staff of the president's office on Oct. 16 in front of Yiniantang, Zhongnanhai (the Middle and South Lake), Beijing.

1923年10月5日国会选举曹锟为大总统。10日曹就职。16日在中南海颐年堂前大总统府指挥处全体职员合影。

On March 2, 1931, the ten-member Committee for Drafting a Provisional Constitution was set up for the coming National Conference in Nanjing. This group photo of the committee was taken on April 8, 1931 at the Temple of Heaven. Some of the esteemed members are Wang Chonghui and Wu Zhihui.

1931年3月2日成立了由王宠惠、吴稚辉等10人组成的约法起草委员会，为将在南京召开的国民会议制定《训政时期的约法》。此图为1931年4月8门约法起草委员会在天坛的合影。

In October 1934, the Thirteenth Dalai Lama, one of Tibetan Buddhism leaders, passed away. The national government sent the special envoy Huang Musong to Tibet to offer sacrifices to him. Here is Huang Musong offering sacrifices in the Potala Palace.

1934年10月，西藏宗教领袖达赖十三世圆寂后，国民政府派黄慕松为专使入藏致祭。图为黄慕松在布达拉宫宗教大厅致祭时的情形。

In an attempt to destroy the Communist forces, Chiang Kai-shek initiated the New Life Movement in the areas around Communist bases in (1934—1937). This picture shows the magistrate of Guiyang County, Guizhou, Li Hou'an (back row, standing in the middle with a baby in his arms), and Miao people at the New Life Movement Conference.

1934—1937年间，蒋介石为配合军事上对中国共产党苏区的围剿，在国统区内开展新生活运动。图为1936年贵州省贵阳新生活运动大会上，贵阳县长李厚安(中立抱幼子者)与参加大会苗族民众的合影。

The Fourth Conference of the Japanese-controlled Joint Commission of the Republican Government of China was ended on March 30, 1939.

1939年3月30日伪"中华民国政府联合委员会"第四次会议闭会时的合影。

The Sixth Conference of the Japanese-controlled Joint Commission of the Republican Government of China on September 21, 1939.

1939年9月21日伪"中华民国政府联合委员会"第六届会议合影。

The Seventh Conference of the Japanese-controlled Joint Commission of the Republican Government of China on December 16, 1939.

1939年12月16日伪"中华民国政府联合委员会"第七届会议合影。

On December 2, 1937, the Xinmin (New Life) Society was founded with Japanese support. Wang Kemin, a Chinese traitor, was commissioned as the first president of the society. His inaugural ceremony was given in Huairentang, Beijing.

1937年12月日本帝国主义扶持华北伪政权成立傀儡组织"新民会"。1939年12月2日大汉奸王克敏出任第一任""新民会"会长,于怀仁堂举行就职典礼。图为王克敏步入会场。

In March 1941, Shiozawa Kiyomuru was commissioned as minister of the Japanese Asian Promotion North China Liaison Office. Shiozawa, seen here, paid a visit to Wang Yitang, chairman of the North China Government Administrative Commission.

1941年3月日本兴亚院华北联络部长官盐泽清室来华就任，拜访伪"华北政务委员会"汉奸头目王揖唐。

On May 27, 1942, Tanabe, vice chief staff of the Japanese Invasion Army paid a visit to Wang Yitang who was president of the Xinmin Society at that time.

1942年5月27日侵华日军田边参谋次长拜访日伪"新民会"会长王揖唐。

On August 10, 1942, Japanese Lieutenant General Wamatsu paid a visit to Wang Yitang (middle), president of the Xinmin Society.

1942年8月10日侵华日军山西军团长岩松中将访问伪"新民会"，与王揖唐(中者)合影。

In October 1942, Wang Yitang paid a visit to Manchukuo and had a talk with the puppet mayor of Xinjing (present Changchun City), Zhang Lianqing.

1942年10月王揖唐访问伪"满洲国"时在新京(今长春)市公署与伪市长张联卿会谈。

In October 1942, the North China Government Delegation led by Wang Yitang paid a visit to Manchukuo. Here is a group photo of Wang Yitang and Umetsu Michiro, Japanese General of the Manchuria Army.

1942年10月伪"华北政务委员会"委员长王揖唐率伪"华北政府代表团"访伪"满洲国",在下榻官邸与日本关东军司令梅津美治郎大将合影。

Wang Yitang and Japanese army officers, October 1942.

1942年10月王揖唐访问"满洲国"时与日本军界人物祝酒。

Before his visit to Japan, Wang Yitang paid a visit to the puppet mayor of Shanghai, Chen Gongbo.

王揖唐赴日访问前在上海与伪"中华民国临时政府"的伪上海市长陈公博会面留影。

When the Fourth Public Security Reinforcement Movement was started, Wang Yitang visited Tianjin. The puppet mayor of Tianjin, Wen Shizhen, met him at the railway station on May 30, 1942.

1942年5月30日王揖唐在日伪第四次治安强化运动时，抵达天津与伪天津市长温世珍在车站合影。

The Japanese Vice Admiral Shimizu paying a visit to Beijing. This group photo was taken in the Navy Mansion, Dingxiang Lane. Front row, left to right: Cao Rulin, Shimizu, Wang Yitang, Wang Kemin and Qi Xieyuan.

驻青岛日本侵华海军北支舰队长官清水中将来北京时与王克敏、王揖唐、齐燮元、曹汝霖合影于丁香胡同海军公馆。前排左起曹汝霖、清水、王揖唐、王克敏、齐燮元。

In May 1942, the North China Government Administrative Commission launched the Fourth Public Security Reinforcement Movement in an attempt to enslave the Chinese people. Here, Wang Yitang is seen inspecting the Zhengding Xinmin Society during the movement.

1942年5月间日伪"华北政务委员会"在华北展开旨在奴化中国人民的第四次治安强化运动。图为伪"新民会"会长王揖唐在运动期间视察伪"新民会"正定总会。

In April 1942, the Xinmin Society held a calligraphy and painting exhibition in Shuixie, Zhongshan Park. Wang Yitang paid a visit to the exhibition.

1942年4月伪"新民会"在北京中央公园水榭举办"兴亚"书画展览会,此系伪"新民会"会长王揖唐参观时留影。

Li Shaowei, governor of Yenching Dao (an administrative district) and leader of the Yenching Dao Quelling Corps which was under the control of the puppet North China Government Administrative Commission.

伪"华北政务委员会"所辖的燕京道道尹兼燕京道区联合讨伐队总队长李少微。

The Magistrate of Gaojin County and Japanese officers in front of Dachengdian, Tongxian County, Beijing.

伪"华北政务委员会"所辖的燕京道高近甲县政等与日军军官及随员在通县大成殿前留影。

The Yenching Dao Quelling Corps giving an address to villagers.

日伪燕京道区联合讨伐队向当地村民训话的情形。

A Japanese immigrant family.

日本"开拓村"中一户移民家庭合影

After the Mukden Incident (September 18, 1931), which led to the Japanese occupation of Northeast China , Japan started a large scale immigration program — the One Million Agricultural Families Immigration to Manchukuo. With government subsidies, Japanese immigration corps containing 200 to 300 families each came to China in large numbers. Statistics revealed that by August 1945, about 100,000 families, over 300,000 Japanese, had immigrate to Northeast China.

1931年"九·一八"事变之后，日本帝国主义在我国东北进行大规模的移民侵略，成立了"海外拓务委员会"、"满洲拓殖股份公司"等机构，制定了《满洲农业移民百万户移驻计划》由日本政府给予集团开拓移民补助费。以200至300户组成"开拓团"或"开拓村"向中国东北大规模移民，据统计，到1945年8月，移入我国东北的日本移民大约为十万户三十万人。本页的四幅图片反映了日本占领东北时建立的移民"开拓村"的生活，移民及村落建设情况。

A Japanese immigrant village in a suburb of Harbin City, 1944.

1944年哈尔滨郊外的日本移民村落建筑情形

A Japanese immigrant village in the Japanese-controlled Binjiang Province. The entrance to the village is built like a blockhouse complete by gun holes.

伪满滨江省"天理村生殖军"(拓殖村)外景。村口城堡一般的大门上，设有射击孔，成为日本在伪"满洲国"统治的堡垒。

The Autumn Worship to Confucius given by the puppet North China Government Administrative Commission in the Confucius Temple, September 10, 1942.

1942年9月10日，伪"华北政务委员会"组织的秋祀孔子大典，此系在孔庙举行演礼时的情形。

On April 30, 1941, the puppet North China Government Administrative Commission organized a parade to celebrate its first anniversary.

1941年4月30日由伪"华北政务委员会"组织的"庆祝国民政府还都暨华北政务委员会成立周年大会"游行的情形。

A grand fair to celebrate the "success" of the Japanese invasion of China was held in Harbin City, 1944.

1944年伪"满洲国"在哈尔滨举办"大东亚战争完遂哈尔滨大博览会"。

The celebration of the first anniversary of the North China Government Administrative Commission was held in front of Taihedian (Hall of Supreme Peace) on April 30, 1941.

1941年4月30日"庆祝国民政府还都暨华北政务委员会成立周年大会"在太和殿集会情形。

In the Japanese-controlled Manchukuo, Confucius was worshipped twice a year. Here is a worship ceremony in 1943.

日本帝国主义控制的伪"满洲国",把一年两次的"祀孔"列为法定祭日。此系1943年伪"满洲国"进行"祀孔"活动的场面。

In April 1945, the Chinese delegation attended the foundation conference of the United Nations. This picture shows Song Ziwen, Chinese foreign minister, addressing the conference.

1945年4月国民政府派代表团出席联合国成立大会。图为国民政府外交部长宋子文在大会上发言。

In May 1948, university students in Beijing held a demonstration against American troops.

1948年5月北京大学生"反美扶日"集会游行,一些军警倍受感动,也参加了集会。

In June 1919, Xu Shuzheng, a subordinate of Duan Qirui, was commissioned to administrate northwest border affairs and supervise the aftermath affairs of Outer Mongolia. The former Kara Korum (today's Ulan Bator) Office was replaced by the Kara Korum Northwest Border Affairs Office.

1919年6月段祺瑞的心腹徐树铮为西北筹边使，执掌西北的军政财务，并督办外蒙古善后一切事宜。裁撤了原设库伦办事大员并将其公署改为库伦西北筹边使公署。此系由原库伦办事大员公署改设的库伦西北筹边使公署外景。

The National Conference was held in the auditorium of the Central University, Nanjing, May 1931.

1931年5月在南京召开的"国民会议"会场——中央大学礼堂。

Taiwan became a Japanese colony following the Sino-Japanese War of 1894. A viceroy was sent by the Japanese government to Taiwan. Here is the viceroy's office in Taipei.

1895年中日甲午战争后台湾沦为日本帝国主义的殖民地，由日本派总督在台湾实行殖民统治。图为设在台北的日本"台湾总督府"全景。

In an attempt to fully occupy China, Japanese invaders instigated the autonomy movement in North China. On November 25, 1935, Yin Rugeng, administrator of Jidong (east Hebei), took the lead in founding the Jidong Anti-Communist Autonomous Government (seen in this picture), which controlled more than 20 counties.

1935年日本帝国主义为配合其对华侵略步伐，积极策动"华北自治"。同年11月25日国民党的冀东行政督察专员、汉奸殷汝耕在通县抢先成立了"冀东防共自治政府"，统辖20余县。图为"冀东防共自治政府"的外景。

The National Government, Nanjing, May 1931.

1931年5月的南京国民政府外景

The presidential residence, Nanjing, January 1935.

1935年1月位于南京的国民政府主席官邸。

Supported by Japanese invaders, Wang Jingwei established the Provisional Government of the Republic of China on March 30, 1940. At the same time, the former North China Provisional Government was replaced by the North China Government Administrative Commission with Wang Kemin acting as chairman.

1940年3月30日在日本帝国主义的扶持下,汪精卫成立"中华民国临时政府",同时,将原伪"华北临时政府"改作"华北政务委员会",由王克敏任委员长,隶属于汪伪"中华民国临时政府"。此系伪"华北政务委员会"外景。

In July 1932, the National Joint Conference was established in Manchukuo. In 1936, it was renamed the Conference of the Manchuria Empire. In addition to a standing committee, it had a National Joint Conference. Here is the National Joint Conference in 1944.

1932年7月,在日本帝国主义的操纵下,成立为实行殖民统治的政治组织—(伪满)全国联合协议会。1936年改称"满洲帝国协和会"。它除了具有常设的机构理事会之外,还有"全国联合协议会"。图所反映的是1944年在伪"满洲帝国协和会"机关所在地召开的伪满"全国联合协议会"会场外景。

The National Joint Conference convened by the Japanese-controlled Conference of the Manchuria Empire.

伪"满洲帝国协和会"召开的"全国联合协议会"会议内部场景

The Supreme Court of Manchukuo in Xinjing (present Changchun).

位于伪满洲国新京(今长春)的"满洲帝国最高法院"的全景

The State Council of Manchukuo in Xinjing (present Changchun).

位于伪满洲国新京(今长春)新建的"满洲帝国国务院"全景

宗教篇

RELIGION

宗教是人类社会生活这棵常青树上开放的不结果实但极为鲜艳的罂粟花。无论是在佛堂道场,抑或基督、天主教堂,一柱袅袅高香,一阵悠扬唱诗,使人仿佛看到了来世,进入了天国;精神得到了安抚,灵魂得到了净化……

但是,宗教作为社会意识形态之一,必然会被打上时代的烙印。旧中国的宗教就被打上了深深的半封建半殖民地的烙印。从本篇精选的图片中,可以非常清晰地看出这一点。

一方面,随着西方列强的入侵,西方传教士的来华传教,中国传统的佛教、道教已失去其在中国的绝对主导地位,在大部分地区都已走向衰落,政治影响和社会影响均大为减弱,尤其是在日本侵华战争爆发以后,日本帝国主义利用佛教对中国进行精神侵略,将其作为奴役中国人民的工具,使中日佛教文化交流蒙上了阴影。

另一方面,随着西方列强的入侵,大量传教士涌入中国,他们在各种不平等条约的保护下,几乎深入到中国每一个角落,广建教堂,发展教徒,对中国政治、社会的影响迅速扩大。

本篇照片大致可分为以下两个部分:

旧中国佛教、道教的状况,包括"中国佛学会"的成立、"居士林"在各地的发展、日本帝国主义在华北组织的"中国佛教学院",等等。

基督教在旧中国的传播,包括传教士的传教和布道活动、教会的教育和慈善事业、中国政府与教会的关系、教会在抗日战争中的一些活动,等等。

Many Chinese people liken religion to a fruitless poppy flower — aesthetically pleasing, but providing little good. In temples or churches, filled with the smells of incense, and melodious songs of praise to God, it seems to the visitors that their souls have entered into Heaven, allowing them to forget all their earthly suffering.

Religion, as a kind of social ideology, is deeply influenced by the time. The religious system in Old China was based on the country's semi-feudal and semi-colonial conditions. When China was forced to open up to the outside world, Western missionaries came to China in the wake of Western battleships. They penetrated nearly every corner of China, and built a great number of Churches under the protection of various unequal treaties. This, in effect, caused China's traditional religions, Buddhism and ·Taoism, to lose some of their followers. Although there were several important events in the world of Chinese Buddhism during this period, such as the foundation of China Buddhist Society, the Jushilin Lay Buddhist Society and the China Buddhist Theological Institute, this traditional religion failed to maintain its original influences on political and social affairs in most areas. Later, during the Sino-Japanese War, Japan made use of Buddhism in an effort to control the spiritual life of the Chinese people.

Special attention is given in this chapter to the spread of Christianity in China and the church's efforts in building schools, charity institutions and its support for China against Japanese invaders.

Buddhist monks having a ve-
getarian dinner, North China,
during the 1930's.

民国时期华北和尚吃斋。

Master Taixu (1890—1947) founded the
Buddhist Association of China in 1921. A
year later, he set up the Wuchang Buddhist Theological Institute, which was
one of the three Buddhist research and
education centers during that period.
Here Master Taixu gives a lecture to his
women students, August 1931.

1921年太虚法师(1890—1947年)
创立"中国佛学会"并任会长。次
年组织成立武昌佛学院,成为近
代中国三大宗教研究和教育的中
心之一。这是1931年8月太虚法师
在北平传授三皈女弟子的情景。

A famous Buddhist
monk Yuanchi, Taiwan.

台原持和尚

Dr. Hocking, a philosophy professor at
Harvard University, and some members of
the Beijing Jushilin Lay Buddhist Society,
April 1932.

1932年4月美国哈佛大学哲学教
授霍金到华北居士林考察时，与
北京居士会会员合影。

The Jushilin Lay Buddhist Society was
first founded in 1918, and was later renamed the World Jushilin Lay Buddhist
Society. During the 1930's, this society
had members in most large cities of China.
Situated at Xi'anmen Street, Beijing, the
North China Jushilin Lay Buddhist Society
was founded in 1930. Here are some
members of the society after their initiation ceremony into monkshood, Nov.
1932. Seated in the middle is Master
Huijue.

清代居士佛教兴起，至民国初年
更盛。1918年出现"居士林"—为
佛教在家信徒举行活动的团体所
建立，后改名为"世界佛教居士
林"，至三十年代发展到全国各大
城市。北平的机关称"华北居士
林"，1930年建立，位于西安门大
街。图为1932年11月华北居士林
第二次授瑜伽菩萨戒纪念摄影。
前排中央者为会觉法师。

The North China Jushilin Lay Buddhist Society celebrating *ullambhana*, the Ghost Festival, on Aug. 14, 1932. Here, students of the a women's Buddhist Theological Institute are learning the Prajnaparamita (Diamond) Sutra.

1932年8月14日华北居士林设盂兰盆会(佛教的活动仪式),女子佛学院何但拔格喇嘛的女弟子在学习金刚经时的情形。

The North China Jushilin Lay Buddhist Society giving a warm welcome to Chiangchia Khutukhtu, a living Buddha, and Yu Jinhe, director of the Peiping Public Security Bureau on Oct. 29, 1933.

1933年10月29日华北居士林欢迎国师章嘉呼图克图及北平市公安局余晋和局长等合影。

Buddhist nuns in Sansheng Convent, toward the end of the Qing Dynasty.

清末三圣庵出家尼姑

Dr. Charles Boynton, an American scholar, had a picture taken after his initiation ceremony into monkshood in the North China Jushilin Lay Buddhist Society.

美国学者包乐登博士在华北居士林受戒后的留影

Chiangchia Living Buddha (1890 — 1957) on his twentieth birthday, 1910. He became the Nineteenth Chiangchia Khutukhtu in 1899. During the reign of Emperor Qianlong, Chiangchia Khutukhtu was made Buddhist leader of the Yellow Sect in the south of the Gobi Desert — Inner Mongolia. In 1928, the Nineteenth Chiangchia was appointed a member of the Mongolian and Tibetan Affairs Commission, and the Central Control Commission.

清宣统二年(公元1910年)，章嘉活佛20岁照片。章嘉本名罗桑班殿丹毕蓉梅(1890—1957)，生于青海，藏族。1899年受封继为章嘉呼图克图十九世。清乾隆时确立章嘉呼图克图主持漠南蒙古黄教，为内蒙佛教的教主。1928年民国政府封其为净觉辅教大师，任民国蒙藏委员、国民党中央监委。

Anchin Khutukhtu, during the 1900's.

清末安钦呼图克图

Japan, to further its imperialistic ambitions, made use of Buddhism to strengthen its control over North China. In March 1940, Beijing Jushilin organized the puppet China Buddhist Theological Institute. Here is the institute's opening ceremony.

1940年3月日本帝国主义利用佛教推行其对中国华北人民的殖民奴役，由北京居士林组织伪中国佛教学院。此系中国佛教学院举行开学典礼摄影。

Musical instruments used in a Mongolian Lamasery.

蒙古喇嘛教寺院的乐器

A Lamaist rite, Mongolia.

蒙古喇嘛僧修行的道场

The Tibetan school sponsored by Beijing Mahabodhi Society, Dec. 8, 1940.

1940年12月8日北京菩提学会藏文讲习所教职学员合影

During the early 1930's, Japan, in hopes of invading North China, made use of Buddhism to rope in former high-ranking officials. This photograph was taken in 1932, when a famous Japanese Buddhist Tanaka Kiyozimi visited China. Front Row: Duan Qirui (second from left). Next to him, right: Tanaka, and Wang Yitang.

20世纪30年代初日本帝国主义为了配合向华北的侵略,利用宗教关系,拉拢华北清朝和北洋军阀的遗老。此系1932年日本中日密教研究会代理总裁田中清纯法师与段祺瑞、王揖唐等人的合影。前排左二段祺瑞,左三田中清纯、左四王揖唐。

The Japanese Buddhist, Tanaka Kiyozimi and members of the Tianjin Jushilin Lay Buddhist Society, June 1937. Seating in front row, left to right: Cao Rulin (third), Tanaka, and Wang Yitang.

1937年6月,日本中日密教研究会代理总裁田中清纯法师在天津与旨在复兴密宗的天津居士林会员的合影。前排就坐的左三为曹汝霖,左四田中清纯,左五王揖唐。

The second anniversary of Chinese Buddhist Theological Institute, March 17, 1942.

1942年3月17日中国佛教学院
第二周年会留影

The grand reception for the ashes of Buddha on April 21, 1945.

1945年4月21日佛教同愿会恭迎
佛舍利

At the Beginning ceremony of the Chinese Buddhist Theological Institute, 1944.

1944年中国佛教学院开学合
影。

Yangzhou Putong Buddhist School, during the early republican era.

民国初年扬州普通僧学堂教师合影

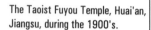

The Taoist Fuyou Temple, Huai'an, Jiangsu, during the 1900's.

清末敕建江苏淮安道教孚佑宫传戒照片

A group photograph of the participants attending the Methodist Church's East Asian Conference. This sect of Christianity entered China in 1847 and built many churches in the east and middle part of China in the following years.

美以美会东亚中央特议会代表合影。该会是基督教教派卫理宗在北美的组织，1847年进入中国传教，相继在华中、江西、华北、华西、福建等地建立教区。

Beijing Catholic Seminary, July 2, 1931.

1931年7月2日天主教北京修道院
全体恭祝惠大院长银庆合影

Pehtang Catholic Cathedral, Beijing, June 1937.

1937年6月北堂200名信教徒合影

Nuns of the Church of St. Joseph, Beijing, 1929.

1929年天主教北平若瑟院修女在
北平宗座代表公署前的合影

The All-China Public Religion Promotion Society held its national conference in Shanghai, 1935. Lu Bohong (right) and Zhu Zhiyao (left) were there elected president and vice-president.

1935年"中华全国公教进行会" 在上海召开全国大会，推举陆伯鸿、朱志尧分别担任正副会长。图为陆伯鸿（右）、朱志尧（左）会议期间的合影。

In 1933, the Vatican made Mario Zanin nuncio to China. Here is Zanin (standing in the middle), addressing the crowd at his welcome meeting, Shanghai.

1933年罗马天主教教廷派蔡宁总主教为教廷驻华代表。图为蔡宁主教（中立披红衣者）在上海各界欢迎大会上发表讲话。

People from the national government and the religious circle meeting Archbishop Mario Zanin at the Shanghai North Railway Station, 1935.

1935年民国政府及宗教界人士在上海北站迎接蔡宁主教。

A group photograph of the staff of the Peiping Catholic Seminary on the fifteenth anniversary of St. Paul's Church on Nov. 3, 1939. This sect was founded by the Vatican in 1885. Its first church in Beijing was constructed in 1924.

1939年11月3日，北平天主教修道院全体人员庆祝成立圣伯多禄善会十五周年合影。该会由罗马教廷于1885年建立，同年来华在陕西传教。1924年在北京建立修道院传教。

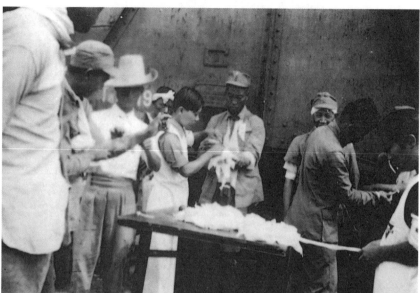

Lei Mingyuan, a Belgian missionary, organized the Mass Service Corps of the North China Battle Field in Shanxi, 1938. He encouraged North China Catholics to join the Anti-Japanese War. Here is the priest addressing the staff of the Kunming Higher Court in June, 1939.

1938年比利时天主教教士雷鸣远在山西组织"华北战地督导民众服务团",并任服务团主任,发动华北天主教徒参加抗战。图为1939年6月雷鸣远神甫在昆明高等法院对全体职工发表抗战演讲时的情形。

The military service corps of the YMCA offering first-aid to wounded soldiers at Guangshui Railway Station, during the Anti-Japanese War.

抗日战争期间全国基督教青年会军人服务部在广水车站医治抗日将士伤病员

Leaders of the military service corps of the YMCA.

抗日战争期间组织全国基督教青年会军人服务部的领导成员合影

Missionaries of the Peiping Pehtang Catholic Cathedral, Feb. 24, 1938.

1938年2月24日天主教北平西什库教堂传教士等祝圣王安国主教合影。

Priests and students of the seminary attached to the Pehtang Catholic Cathedral in the late Qing Dynasty.

清末北京天主教北堂所属的修道院全体学生与传教士合影。

The Children's Seminary attached to the Pehtang Catholic Cathedral.

清末北京天主教北堂所属的儿童修道院全体合影

Bishops and believers of the Pehtang Catholic Cathedral.

清末北京西什库教堂的主教与信徒合影

Peiping Catholic Church offering relief to poor children.

北平天主教会救济穷苦儿童。

Students at a girls' primary school sponsored by the Catholic Church of Wen'an County, June 1938.

1938年6月文安县天主教堂所属的自立女子小学学员合影

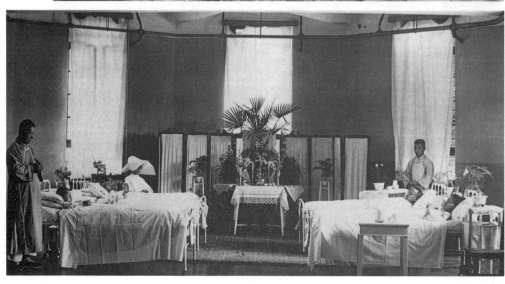

A hospital opened by the Catholic Church, Peiping.

北平教会开设的医院病房内景

Priests and students at the Pehtang Catholic Theological Seminary, Sept. 1934.

1934年9月北堂神学院师生与惠大院长(中坐者)合影

The bishop and his followers at the Pehtang Catholic Cathedral, Beijing, 1892.

1892年北京天主教西什库教堂所属的主教与教徒合影

A Catholic theological seminary in Zhuozhou County in 1933-1934.

1933—1934年，天主教涿县城内朋道学院师生合影

The bishop and priests at the Pehtang Catholic Cathedral, Beijing, toward the end of Qing Dynasty.

清末北京西什库教堂主教与神甫的合影

Foreign missionaries in Manchu clothes, 1909.

1909年穿着清代服装的传教士合影

Bishops in China, in the early republican period.

民国初年各地主教神甫合影

A grand ceremony of the Catholic Church during the 1930's.

民国时期天主教会举行盛典。

Bishops attending a meeting in Tianjin, during the late Qing Dynasty.

清末天津外省教会会长集会合影

China's bishops during the 1900's.

清末在华主教合影

The Russian Orthodox Nicole Church,
Harbin City.

哈尔滨俄国东正教尼古拉堂

A Catholic church built in Dahan Village,
Langfang, post 1900.

1900年以后新建的廊房大韩村天
主教堂

A Catholic church, Haibei.

设在海北的天主教堂

In order to extend the Middle and South
Lakes, an exquisite imperial garden, the
Qing government offered 450,000 taels
of silver to move the French Catholic
Church at Canshikou to Xishiku, inside
the Xi'anmen. Here is Xishiku (or Pehtang)
Catholic Church.

清末清朝政府为扩建中南海西
岸,将法国天主教蚕池口教堂(老
北堂)迁移至西安门内西什库,即
新建西什库教堂(新北堂),并给移
建费45万两白银。此系清末的西
什库教堂院内仁慈堂正面

The Wanghailou Church, Tianjin, after its second reconstruction in 1897. Later it was burnt during the Boxer Uprising of 1900.

1897年第二次重新修建的天津望海楼教堂。此堂于1900年义和团运动中被焚毁。

The Zhuozhou Catholic Church after its reconstruction, post 1900.

1900年后重新修建的天主教涿州教堂

A missionary school during the 1900's.

清末教会学校大门口

Western missionaries in Chinese clothes setting out to spread their religious faith.

清末西方传教士,身着中国服装,乘坐马车外出传教。

In 1945, the Vatican appointed Tian Gengxin as the Archbishop of Peiping to administrate the religious affairs in China. He was the first Chinese-born cardinal in the Far East. Here is the Cardinal Tian Gengxin (seated in the middle), and believers in Mentouguo, Peiping, May 1948.

1945年罗马教廷任命天主教青岛主教田耕辛为有史以来远东的第一位华籍红衣主教,并任命他为北平总主教,主持全国教务。此系田耕辛枢机主教1948年5月在北平门头沟时与欢迎众教徒的合影。前排中坐者即田耕辛。

Baldus Jean Henri (or An Ruowang, 1814 — 1889), a French missionary, came to China in 1835. Four years later he settled in Henan Province and was later appointed by the Vatican to be the first nuncio to Henan. In 1865, he was moved to Jiangxi and later died in Jiujiang.

安若望(1814—1889)，法国遣使会教士，1835年来华，1839年到河南，1864年被选为首任罗马教皇驻河南代表，1865年调往江西，后死于九江。

Bary Geraud (or Bai Zhenduo, 1825 — 1905).

白振铎(1825—1905)，法国遣使会教士

Bishop Ogilvie. 奥科贝尔斯主教

Bishop Bernard. 伯纳德主教

军事篇

MILITARY

　　战争的硝烟一直充斥着旧中国的历史,民族战争与军阀之间的混战、正义的与非正义的战争连年不绝。

　　1840年的鸦片战争中,大清政府的大刀长矛、土枪土炮败在了西方列强的坚船利炮之下,军事上面的悬殊震惊了中国的有识之士,他们开始学习西方的军事制度,引进制造先进武器的机器设备,实行新式的西方军事教育,这一切,促成了旧中国从传统军事向近代军事的重大转变,诞生了新式的陆、海军。

　　但是,从清王朝到北洋军阀政府,再到国民党政府,旧中国政治腐败这一痼疾无法根治,因而军事制度、装备、教育的近代化也就不能彻底,也就不能改变旧中国被侵略、被蹂躏的命运,也就不能结束军阀混战、割据的局面。

　　本篇选录的这组照片,从三个方面展现了旧中国的军事概况:

　　清末中国军事的近代化:包括军队编制、军事设备、军事教育的状况;

　　旧中国的近代化军队是专制统治镇压国内人民革命的工具,如宣统三年(1911年)校阅禁卫军,向人民示威;或成为军阀混战割据的工具,如1918年段祺瑞借款督办参战军,扩充实力,试图用武力统一南方;

　　列强的侵华战争:包括八国联军的侵华战争、日本帝国主义的侵华战争;

　　此外,还收录了抗战胜利后,美军、国民党军和共产党军队三方组成的"军调处"的一些活动的照片,从这些照片中,既可以嗅到酝酿战争的紧张气氛,又可以感觉到全国人民要求停战、渴望和平的心态。

　　Warfare was almost constantly present in Old China. During the Opium War of 1840, the Qing troops, armed with swords and spears, were defeated brutally by the powerful battleships of the Western powers. The Chinese people were shocked by the military might of the West. Some Chinese began to study the military systems of the West, introduce advanced weapons and machines, and set up Western military academies. The renovations led to the birth of a modern infantry and navy for China. In Old China, however, the army was used by the warlords to suppress popular rebellion, or to build personal power base. From the Qing Dynasty to the post-1911 governments, the incurable political corruption impeded a complete and rapid military modernization. Without a strong and unified army, China could not free herself from being invaded by the imperialist powers and from the brutal clutches of the warlords.

　　This chapter also pays special attention to the Executive Headquarters for Military Mediation — an organization set up after the victory in the Anti-Japanese War by representatives from the US, the Kuomintang and the Chinese Communist Party in an effort to prevent a possible civil war.

After the allied forces of the eight powers invaded Beijing in 1900, Qing rulers renovated the government administration and organized a Western-style army. The New Army, as it was named, composed of the regular army, continuance army and reserves. Here are officers of a continuance army in Jiangsu Province.

1900年八国联军侵华战争后,清政府推行"新政",编练新式军队。1904年,清政府正式划定新练军队军制,分为常备军、续备军和后备军三等。图为由江苏抚标改编后的续备亲兵中营长官合影。

In 1900, the Qing government organized the New Army. By the end of 1911, two military regions in the area south of the Yangtze River were being guarded by the New Army. Here is an artillery unit of the New Army.

1900年后清朝政府编练新式军队，截止1911年，江南练成新军二镇。图为江南常备新军炮队官兵及其装备。

A breech-loading artillery built for the New Army at Shiziling, Wusong.

清末清朝政府编练新式军队时，在吴淞狮子岭配备的八百磅后膛钢炮。

A breech-loading artillery built for the New Army at Lanjiangji, Anhui.

清朝政府编练新式军队时，在安徽拦江矶新配备的新式九十六磅万斤后膛炮。

Officers and soldiers of the New Army guarding the Shiziling Fort, Wusong, Jiangsu.

清朝政府编练新式军队后，配置在江苏吴淞狮子岭炮台的新军官兵。

Officers and soldiers of the Xiangwei Regular Army, Hunan.

清朝政府编练新式军队时，新编成的湖南湘威常备军统领和官兵合影。

A torpedo ship crew of the Jiangnan Navy.

清朝政府编练新式军队时，新编练的江南水师鱼雷艇官兵。

The military band established in Shanxi in the late Qing Dynasty.

清朝末年山西新建的陆军军乐队

Anhui Military Academy founded toward the end of the Qing Dynasty. Here are instructors and the school's first graduating class.

清朝末年设立的安徽武备学堂教习头班毕业学生合影

When the Qing government organized the New Army, several military academies were founded by local governments to train senior officers. Here are instructors of the Jiangnan Officers' Academy in Nanjing.

清政府在编练新式军队时，为培养高级军事人才，在一些地方设立军事学堂。图为设在南京的江南将备学堂官长教习合影。

Russo-Japanese War, which erupted over gains in Northeast China, broke out in 1904—1905. Here is the Japanese headquarters for the war in Fengtian.

1904—1905年间，日本与俄国为争夺在中国东北的利益，爆发了日俄战争。图为战争期间日军驻奉天的司令部。

In the early days of 1911, the Qing Government sent Zai Xun and other high-ranking officials to inspect the Beiyang Army in an effort to tighten the control over the army as well as to show off military forces. Here are the inspecting officials, left to right: Yin Chang, Zai Sou, Zai Xun, Yi Shou, Zai Tao, Lin Gong, Bai Wang and Tai Xueheng.

1911年初，清朝政府为了加强对新建陆军(北洋军)的控制，检阅新编练的军队，炫耀清朝的军事力量，派大臣载洵等校阅陆军。图为出任的校阅陆军大臣合影。左起荫昌、载搜、载洵、奕寿、载涛、麟公、帕王、谭学衡。

Zai Feng, the prince regent, inspecting imperial guards at the military drill grounds outside Deshengmen, Beijing in March 1911.

1911年3月校阅陆军时，摄政王载沣在德胜门外教场校阅禁卫军的情况。

The police bureau of Guizhou Province founded in 1907.

1907年贵州全省巡警开局留影

The newly trained police in Anhui Province.

清朝政府编练新军时,新编成的
安徽警察官兵合影。

The newly trained police in Jiujiang, Jiangxi Province.

清末编练新军时,新编成的
江西九江警察官兵合影。

In 1902, Yuan Shikai established the first police bureaus in Tianjin. In 1905, the Qing government set up the Police Headquarters. Here is the General Police Bureau of Tianjin in the late Qing Dynasty.

1902年袁世凯在天津设立南、北
段巡警局,创办近代中国警察制
度。1905年清政府成立巡警部。图
为清朝末年天津巡警总局外景。

In 1900, the allied forces captured Beijing and stationed themselves in the Imperial Palace. Here are allied troops lining up outside the palace.

1900年八国联军侵华战争中，攻入北京城，进驻紫禁城。图为八国联军列队于紫禁城午门外。

The newly organized army in Guangdong Province.

清朝政府编练新式军队时，新编成的广东陆军操练情形。

The Qing government ordered provincial governments to build military schools. The photograph below shows Bao Fen, governor of Shanxi Province, inspecting the Shanxi Army School in 1905.

清朝政府为培养新式军事人才，规定在京师及各省建立陆军小学堂。图为1905年山西巡抚宝棻视察山西陆军小学堂与学生合影。

寶大帥巡撫山西閱校陸軍小學學堂班卒學生撮影紀念

A group photograph of officers of the allied forces, Qing officials, and foreign missionaries outside the Pehtant Catholic Cathedral.

八国联军军官与清朝官员及外国传教士在北堂合影

During the Sino-Japanese War of 1894, French troops were assembled in Beijing on the pretext of protecting churches and French citizens. The photograph above shows French naval troops gathering in Beijing.

1895年中日甲午战争期间，法国公使以保护教堂及侨民为由，调法国军队进驻北京。图为调入北京的德卡尔特水兵分队官兵合影。

On October 1917, in an effort to extend his personal power and show off military force, Duan Qirui, head of the Anhui Faction in warlords government, inspected the army which was organized to participate World War I. The photograph below shows the troops marching out of Xinhuamen.

1917年10月10日，段祺瑞借用参加第一次世界大战协约国获得的"参战款"组建"参战军"，扩充北洋皖系的势力，以图武力统一南方。是日，为炫耀北洋武力，举行检阅参战军仪式。图为赴南苑参加大阅兵的部队出新华门。

Rest tents were erected for foreign diplomatic envoys during the Nanyuan Inspection on October 10, 1917. The officer with a sword is Admiral Liu Guanxiong.

1917年10月10日中国参战军在南苑大检阅时，参加检阅的外国使节休息区。佩剑穿海军服者为海军总长刘冠雄。

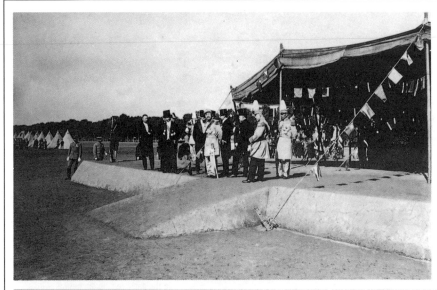

On October 10, 1917, Duan Qirui, along with foreign diplomatic envoys, inspected the army which was organized to participate the First World War at Nanyuan, Beijing.

1917年10月10日段祺瑞及各国使节在北京南苑参战军大阅兵的检阅台上。

Duan Qirui inspecting the cavalry.

1917年10月10日段祺瑞等骑马检阅参加南苑大检阅的骑兵方阵。

During World War I, China was a member of the victorious Entente countries. In November 1918, a grand ceremony to celebrate the victory was held in front of Taihemen (Gate of Supreme Harmony) of the Imperial Palace.

1918年11月第一次世界大战结束，中国作为取得胜利的协约国一员，在北京故宫太和门前举行庆祝协约国胜利大会。图为大会检阅参战军队列的情形。

The anti-contraband police, Linpu, Hebei, in the early republican period.

民国初年河北临浦缉私兵(缉私警察)

A police office in Altaimian, Mongolia, during Manchukuo period. 伪满时期的蒙古阿尔泰面警察署

The anti-contraband police, Cangzhou, Hebei, in the early republican period.

民国初年河北沧州盐沱缉私营官兵驻所

The East Sichuan Police Battalion. This photograph was taken in 1910 when the battalion guarded the First East Sichuan Trade Fair.

1910年间的川东巡警营。图为该巡警营在担负第一次川东劝业会警卫时的合影。

The Public Security Bureau of Minquan County, Henan, established on Nov. 10, 1928.

1928年11月10日河南省民权县公安局开创合影

Japanese troops stationed in Changchun attacked Fort Nanling in the wake of the Mukden Incident (Sept. 18, 1931). Chinese troops were forced to withdraw and soon Japanese troops captured Changchun City. Above is the Nanling Battlefield. When the picture was taken, Nanling was occupied by Japanese troops.

"南岭事件"发生地。1931年9月19日,长春日军为配合"九·一八"日军在沈阳的军事行动,向驻扎在南岭的中国军队发动进攻,经过激战,中国军队被迫撤退,日军长驱直入,占领长春。图为南岭战场,此时已成为日军的驻扎营房。

In the Russo-Japanese War (1904-1905), Japanese troops destroyed the Russian-built North Fort on the Eastern Jiguan Mountain, Lushun.

1904—1905年日俄战争期间,被日军摧毁的中国旅顺东鸡冠山北炮台残景。该炮台为俄国军队修建。

The Japanese police garrison at Batong-guan, Taiwan, during the period of Japanese colonization.

日殖时期的台湾八通关日本警察驻所

The Japanese police garrison at Wushe, Taiwan.

日殖时期台湾雾社附近的日本警察驻所

The Japanese Infantry Espionage Agency set up in Lianyungang, Jiangsu, after the start of the Sino-Japanese War in 1937.

1937年日本侵华战争爆发后的江苏连云港"大日本陆军特务机关"门前。

In 1937 Japanese troops created a series of disturbances on the outskirts of Peiping, revealing Japan's designs to occupy North China. The No. 29 Corps stationed in Peiping prepared for the war actively under the command of Song Zheyuan, seen here saluting his soldiers.

1937年，日本军队在北平一带不断制造事端，欲图侵略华北。驻守在北平的宋哲元二十九军，积极备战。图为宋哲元(行军礼者)检阅备战中的部队。

Before the Marco Polo Bridge Incident (July 7, 1937) soldiers of the No. 29 Corps were prepared in full battle gear to safeguard the bridge.

1937年"七·七"事变前夕，驻守在宛平芦沟桥附近的宋哲元二十九军冯治安部的士兵严阵以待。

Chinese troops on alert during the Songhu Battle in August 1937.

1937年8月开始的淞沪会战中，中国军队严守要道。

The China Medical College, located in Chengdu, was bombed on June 17, 1940. Here are the remains of school buildings after the air attack.

1940年6月17日，位于成都的中国医学院被日机轰炸，校舍遭到毁坏。

The North Railway Station of Shanghai was devastated during the Songhu Battle.

淞沪会战中，上海北站月台路轨被毁。

Japanese troops landing on the coast of China, 1940.

1940年日军某部乘登陆艇在中国海滩登陆。

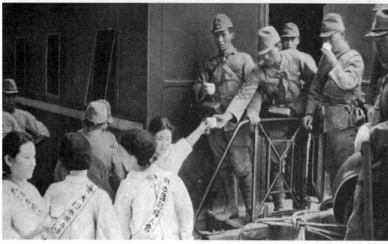

Japanese women greeting Japanese soldiers who had fought on the Peiping-Kweisui Battlefield, 1937.

1937年在平绥战线上，日本国防妇人会慰问日军情形。

Huailai County captured by Japanese troops, 1937.

1937年平绥战线日军攻入怀来县城。

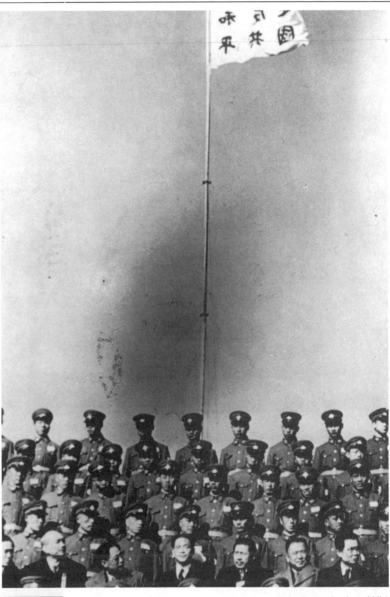

Wang Jingwei (front row in the middle), the Chinese traitor during the Sino-Japanese War of 1937-45, inspecting his puppet army in Shanghai, October 1939.

1939年10月，日本帝国主义扶持的伪政府在上海检阅傀儡军时与汪精卫(前排中者)合影。

Japanese troops training in Peiping during the Sino-Japanese War.

抗日战争时期，日军在占领地北平训练的情形。

Chinese youth brigades fought bravely in the Songhu Battle.

淞沪会战中勇敢的童子军战地服务工作。

The air force of Kuomintang. 待命出发杀敌抗日的国民党空军。

During the Songhu Battle, women volunteers were trained to give first-aid to wounded soldiers.

淞沪会战中，女子救护队加紧练习。

The Buddhist monks' first-aid team served on the battle field actively in August 1937.

1937年8月活跃在淞沪会战战地的上海市僧侣救护队。

A Japanese ammunition ship sunk by Chinese troops.

"抗战"中日军运输军火的轮船被中国军队击沉。

On the second anniversary of the Marco Polo Bridge Incident, people from Yunnan Province, regardless of social class, donated large sums of money to support the war.

"七·七"两周年纪念时,抗战后方云南省各界开展为支援抗日前线的献金活动盛况。

A South Asian overseas Chinese delegation returned to the motherland to convey greetings and appreciation to fighting soldiers. The photograph was taken on March 30, 1940, when the delegation arrived at Yunnan.

1940年3月30日,南洋华侨回国慰问团抵达云南在汽车站留影。

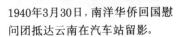

Officials of the Japanese-supported puppet government inspecting their troops in October 1939, Shanghai.

1939年10月日本帝国主义扶持的伪政府在上海检阅傀儡军。

日本降使呈遞降書

On August 15, 1945, Japan declared its surrender in the Pacific War. In Nanjing, on September 9, Chinese officials received Japan's unconditional surrender.

1945年8月15日，日本宣布在第二次世界大战中战败，无条件投降。图为9月9日在南京举行的中国战场日军投降受降仪式中，日本降使向中国政府呈递降书。

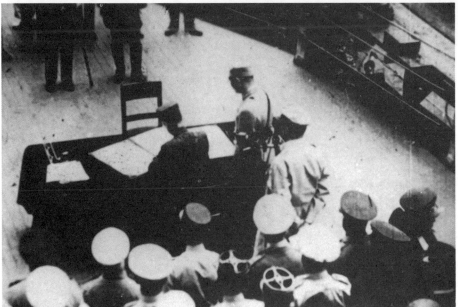

He Yingqing, as the official representative of the Chinese government, accepts Japan's unconditional surrender, September 9, 1945.

1945年9月9日南京受降仪式中，中国政府派何应钦代表蒋介石签受降书。

Xu Yongchang signs the agreement to bring the war to a close aboard a US battleship in Tokyo Harbor, September 2, 1945.

1945年9月2日，第二次世界大战结束后，中国政府代表徐永昌将军在东京美国米苏里号军舰上参加接受日本投降的受降典礼，在日本投降书上签字。

The Japanese Emperor's liaison Shigemitsu Mamoru aboard the US battleship, preparing to sign Japan's Terms of Surrender on Sept. 2, 1945.

1945年9月2日，日本天皇签降代表重光葵等抵达米苏里号军舰待命签字。

Chiang Kai-shek examining the Japan's Terms of Surrender.

1945年抗日战争胜利后，蒋介石审视日本投降书。

Chiang Kai-shek walking on the street in celebration of the victory in the Anti-Japanese War, August 1945.

1945年8月抗日战争胜利后，蒋介石步行重庆街头与民众合影。

A group photo of Zhou Enlai (in Western suit) and American officers working for the Executive Headquarters for Military Mediation, 1946.

1946年周恩来(中间穿西装者)与军调部美方人员在机场留影。

George Marshall inspecting Communist troops at Yan'an Airport in July 1946. Left to Right: Chairman Mao Zedong, Zhou Enlai, Marshall, Zhang Zhizhong and Zhu De.

1946年7月马歇尔在延安机场检阅部队。左起毛泽东、周恩来、马歇尔、张治中、朱德。

Officers of the Executive Headquarters for Military Mediation examining a destroyed railroad, 1946.

1946年军调部人员巡视被破坏的铁路。

外交篇

FOREIGN AFFAIRS

自从十九世纪中叶西方列强借助坚船利炮强行撞开中国国门,传统的所谓"羁縻柔远"已是一厢情愿。旧中国的外交活动可算频繁,但它们在很大程度上带有被迫的性质,所以也就基本没有平等与尊严可言。回顾鸦片战争直至1949年百年间的中国外交史,我们看到的是一次次屈尊、遭辱,和一个个不平等的条约。

本篇精选近五十幅照片,粗略展示了旧中国的种种外交活动,大致可分为以下几个方面:

关于出访:如1868年中国第一个出使欧美的使团——蒲安臣使团;1905年端方等赴东西洋多国考察宪政;1909年载洵等赴欧美考察军政等等;

关于中外交涉:如1900年德国太子来华访问;1922年英国皇太子访问香港;抗日战争时期印度、缅甸代表团访华等等;1900年清政府与八国联军进行的《辛丑条约》的谈判;1914年中俄恰克图谈判等等;

关于中国参加的国际会议:如1926年参加关税会议;1945年参加联合国会议等等;

关于日本侵华战争时期华北伪政府与日、德勾结的照片也收录在此篇。

除上述几项外,本篇还收录了一些反映清末上层贵族家眷与外国人的私交,以及民国时期一些外交礼节性活动的照片。

During the mid-19th century, the Western powers pried open the doors of China with their battleships. Traditional foreign policy was no longer an option for China. The diplomatic relations in Old China, having little equality and dignity, were largely manipulated by foreign powers. In a period of just a hundred years, from the Opium War in 1840 to the establishment of the People's Republic of China in 1949, the history of Old China was filled with humiliations and unequal treaties.

The Foreign Affairs Chapter contains about 50 historical photographs, giving a general overview to the diplomatic activities during that period which include: official visits, diplomatic intercourse international conferences

Also included in this chapter are collusion of Japan, Germany and the puppet North China Government during World War II, personal friendship among the esteemed families and foreigners in the late Qing Dynasty, and some diplomatic protocol affairs during the republican era.

In 1909, Zai Xun (front row, second from left) and Sa Zhenbing (second row, second from left) paid a visit to Western countries to investigate their navies.

1909年载洵、萨镇冰等赴欧美考察海军期间与洋人合影。前排左二载洵,第二排左二萨镇冰。

In 1868, the Qing government sent its first diplomatic mission, which was led by the American diplomat Burlingame Anson (also known as Pu Anchen). Here are members of the Burlingame Mission, left to right: Zhuang Chunling, Gui Rong, Lian Fang, Feng Yi, Champs Emile'de, Sun Jiagu, Burlingame Anson, Zhi Gang, Brown John Mcleavy, De Yi, Take Shina.

1868年清朝政府派出的第一个由洋人率队的正式外交使团—蒲安臣使团的合影，左起庄椿龄、桂荣、联芳、凤仪、德善、孙家谷、蒲安臣、志刚、柏卓安、德彝、塔克什纳、元廷镛、亢砚农。

Duan Fang and foreign envoys with their wives.

端方与外国使节及其夫人的合影

In 1905, the Qing government sent five high-ranking officials including Zai Ze, Dai Hongci and Duan Fang to foreign countries to investigate their political systems. Dai Hongci and Duan Fang paid a visit to America, Germany, Italy and Austria. Here is a group photo of Dai Hongci, Duan Fang and German officials.

1905年清朝政府派载泽、戴鸿慈、端方等五大臣出洋考察政治，史称"五大臣出洋"。其中戴鸿慈、端方前往美、德、意、奥诸国。图为戴鸿慈、端方等在德国与德军政官员的合影。前排坐者自左至右：荫昌、端方、戴鸿慈。

In 1909, Zai Xun paid a visit to Western countries to investigate their navies.

1909年载洵等赴欧美考察海军时,参观德海军设备。

Foreign envoys with their wives and children. The photograph was taken after the signing of the Treaty of 1900.

庚子条约签定后各国外交使节及其夫人、子女的合影。

In 1905, the American special envoy to investigate the silver situation Jenks Jeremiah Whipple came to China. Here is a group photograph of the American envoy and Manchu officials of the Ministry of Foreign Affairs. Front row, left to right are Conger Edwin Hund (American Ambassador in China), Rong Qing, Lu Chuanlin, Jenks, Nantong (foreign minister), Chen Bi. Second row: Shao Ying (second from left). Next to him right Xu Shichang. The right four (left to right): Lei Putong, Rui Feng, Shi Zhaoji and Zhang Yunyan.

1905年美国银价特使精奇来华,与清朝外务部尚书那桐等官员合影。第一排左起美国驻华公使康格、荣庆、鹿传霖、精奇、那桐、陈璧,第二排左二绍英、左三徐世昌、左五雷谱桐、左六瑞丰、左七施肇基、左八张允言。

The crown prince of Germany in China. The Qing officials in the photograph below (left to right) are Lian Fang, Zai Zhen, Yi Kuang, Wu Tingfang, Zai Feng, Qu Hongji, Cheng' Zunyao, and Na Tong. Standing in the middle wearing a sword is the German prince.

1904年4月德国太子访华时 ，庆亲王奕劻与德国太子合影。图中清朝官员左起：联芳、载振、奕劻、伍廷芳、载沣、瞿鸿机、程遵尧、那桐。前排中间挎剑者为德国太子。

In April 1904, the crown prince of Germany paid a visit to China and was received by the Qing Emperor Guangxu. Here is a group photograph of Qing officials and the German prince. Front row, from the second, left to right: Na Tong, Qu Hongji, Yi Kuang, the Prince, Wu Ting-fang, Zai Feng, Munn (German Envoy in China), Cheng Zunyao, and Lian Fang.

1904年4月德国太子访华，受到光绪皇帝接见。图为庆亲王奕劻等赴德驻华使馆时与德国太子合影，图中清朝官员左第二人起那桐、瞿鸿机、奕劻、伍廷芳、载沣、程遵尧、联芳、中间立者为德太子，载沣右为德国驻华公使穆默。

Philip, a German prince consort, paid a visit to China in March 1905. The Manchu government awarded him an honorary title. The group photograph above includes Prince Philip (front row, third from right), Mumm (front row, first from right, German Envoy to China), Yi Kuang (the Prince of Qing), Zai Feng (the Price of Chun), Nan Tong, Hu Yufang, Wu Ting Fang, and Lian Fang.

1905年3月德国亲王利物浦来华，清朝政府授予头等第二双龙宝星。图为利物浦在德国驻华公使穆默陪同下，与庆亲王奕劻等人合影。内有庆亲王奕劻、醇亲王载沣、那桐、胡遹芳、伍廷芳、联芳。前排右一为穆默，右三为德国亲王利物浦。

Wife of Zai Ze and her son with a foreign envoy's wife.

清末载泽夫人偕其子与外国使节夫人合影。

A group photograph of the younger sister of Shan Qi (the prince of Su) and young Japanese women.

清末肃亲王善耆之妹与日本青年妇女合影。

Wife of Zai Ze in Western clothes and a foreign envoy's wife in Manchu clothes.

清末载泽夫人身着洋装与身着旗装的外国人合影。

A group photograph of the younger sister of Shan Qi and a foreign envoy's wife with her children.

清末肃亲王善耆之妹与外国使节夫人及其子女合影。

A group photograph of Manchu officials Zai Xun, Zai Tao, Zai Feng, Zai Zhen, Na Tong, Xu Shichang, Qu Hongji, Yuan Shikai and Japanese, Russian and German officers.

载洵、载涛、载沣、载振、那桐、徐世昌、瞿鸿机、袁世凯等人与日、俄、德军官合影。

Officials of the Ministry of Foreign Affairs Hu Weide, Na Tong, Yi Kuang and Cao Rulin in the third year of the Xuantong Reign of the Qing Dynasty (1911).

宣统三年(1911年)胡惟德、那桐、奕劻、曹汝霖等外务部全体同仁合影。

The Manchu government appointed Zai Xun and Sa Zhenbing as officials to rebuild the navy in 1909. In the same year, a delegation, led by Zai Xun, paid a visit to western countries and Japan to investigate their military systems. Here are Zai Xun and his delegation with Japanese high-ranking officers. Manchu officials are (front row, left to right) Feng Shu (second), Cao Ruying (third), Zhou Ziqi (fourth), Sa Zhenbing (sixth), Zai Xun (seventh), Wang Daxie (eighth), Zheng Rucheng (eleventh).

1909年清朝政府为重振海军,命载洵、萨镇冰为筹办海军大臣。同年载洵率代表团赴欧美及日本考察军务。图为载洵等在日本考察时与日本军界要员的合影。前左二冯恕、左三曹汝英、左四周自齐、左六萨镇冰、左七载洵、左八汪大燮、左十一郑汝成。

After the success of the Wuchang Uprising on Oct. 10, 1911, which lead to the downfall of the Qing Dynasty, the Hubei Military Government was founded. At the same time the Department of Foreign Affairs, headed by Hu Ying, was set up. In Jan. 1912, the Nanjing Provisional Government was founded, as was the Ministry of Foreign Affairs. In April of the same year, the ministry was moved to Beijing. Here are officials of the Department of Foreign Affairs.

1911年10月10日武昌起义后,建立湖北军政府,成立外交司,司长为胡英。1912年1月南京临时政府成立,成立外交部。同年4月临时政府外交部迁往北京。此系1912年4月临时政府北迁时,湖北军政府外交司全体职员合影。

In 1913, the Republic of China was officially recongnized. Here is a group photograph of foreign minister Sun Baoqi (seated in the middle, front row), and foreign diplomats. Front row, left to right: envoys from Belgium, Spain, Sweden, and Russia. Second row: envoys from Denmark, Japan, France, Germany, and the UK. Third row: envoys from Holland, the USA, Portugal, Mexico, and Italy.

1913年各国政府正式承认中华民国,此系孙宝琦外长同各国外交官合影,前排中坐者为孙宝琦。第一排左起为比、西、瑞典、俄公使。第二排为丹、日、法、德、英公使。第三排为荷、美(芮思施)、葡、墨、意公使。

Duan Qirui, president of the provisional republican government, and envoys from France and Belgium in 1926.

1926年中华民国临时执政段祺瑞招待法、比公使合影。

Liang Shiyi and foreign guests in the early years of the Republic of China.

民国初年梁士诒与外宾合影。

影摄體全部交外月九年九国民

Officials of the Ministry of Foreign Affairs in 1920. Fifteen from left, front row is the then foreign minister Yan Huiqing.

1920年民国政府外交部全体同仁合影。左起第十五人为当时的外交总长颜惠庆。

The Living Buddha of Outer Mongolia and his Russian advisors.

外蒙古活佛与俄国顾问合影。

Members of the business community of Hong Kong held a banquet to welcome the Crown Prince of England in April 1922.

1922年4月香港商界举行宴会欢迎英国太子访港。

The Crown Prince of England received a warm welcome in Hong Kong, April 1922.

1922年4月英国皇太子访问香港时,接受各界人士欢迎。

Hong Kong children welcoming the Prince.

欢迎英国皇太子队伍中的香港儿童

Xu Yongchang, governor of Hebei Province, and the Japanese Industrial Investigation delegation, 1929.

1929年河北省省长徐永昌招待日本实业考察团合影。

In Oct. 1925, the Tariff Conference was held in Beijing. Delegates from eleven countries including America, France, England, Japan and Russia attended the conference, which focused on such problems as tariff autonomy for China and customs tariff. The Chinese representatives were Duan Qirui and foreign minister Shen Ruilin. But the conference ended without any results in July 1926.

1926年关税会议中,中国代表招待各国代表。1925年10月此会议在中国北京举行,参加者有美、法、英、日、俄等十一国代表,中国代表为段祺瑞和内阁外交总长沈瑞麟。会上提出和讨论了中国关税自主及税率问题。此会于1926年7月之后,不了了之。

Zhang Xueliang entertaining a diplomatic mission.

张学良招待外交使团合影。

In Aug. 1939, the Indian Nationalist Party Delegation, led by Jawaharlal Nehru, paid a visit to China to discuss Sino-Indian cooperation, and other common concerns with Chiang Kai-shek. Here is a group photograph of Chiang Kai-shek, his wife Song Meiling and Nehru.

1939年8月尼赫鲁率印度国大党代表团访华,在重庆与蒋介石会谈,讨论中印合作及亚洲问题。此系蒋介石、宋美龄夫妇与尼赫鲁合影。

The Sino-British Friendship Society held a send-off party for the British ambassador Cadogan on March 26, 1936.

1936年3月26日中英教谊社欢送英国大使贾德斡合影。左起第八人为贾德斡。

In Dec. 1939, the Japanese official Kuhara Fusanosuke paid a visit to the puppet North China Provisional Government and took a photo with Wang Kemin and Wang Yitang.

1939年12月日本政友会久厚总裁、前外省大臣芳泽来伪华北临时政府时与王克敏、王揖唐等合影。

A group photo of some North China trai-tors with the Japanese on Oct. 15, 1937. Some of them are (front row): Jin Yun-peng (second from left), Qi Xieyuan (fourth from left), next to him, right, Gao Lingwei. Back row: Cao Rulin (second from left) and Wang Yitang (fourth from left).

1937年10月15日华北汉奸头目与日本人合影。前排左二靳云鹏、左四齐燮元、左五高凌慰;后排左二曹汝霖、左四王揖唐。

A group photograph of members of the Japanese-controlled Government Ad-ministrative Commission of Hebei and Chahar Provinces with Japanese officers, 1936. Some of those shown are Zhang Zizhong (fourth from left, front row) puppet governor of Tianjin, Wang Yitang (fourth from left, second row), next to him right Cao Rulin.

1936年伪冀察政务委员会部分委员与日本军将领的合影。前排左四为伪天津市长张自忠。二排左四王揖唐,左五曹汝霖。

In early summer of 1937, Wang Yitang gave a dinner to welcome the Japanese official Onotera in Ningyuan, Tianjin.

1937年夏初,王揖唐等人于天津宁园中设宴为小野寺中将洗尘留影。

王揖唐等人与日本军、政、经巨头合影。前排左起大藏大臣石渡庄太郎、伪华北政务委员会实务总长岳开先、日本制铁取缔役理事会长平生全八三郎、日本银行总裁结成丰太郎、兴亚院华北联络部长官森冈卓、伪华北政务委员会委员长王揖唐、日本经济联监会长乡诚之助、"北支那"开发总裁贺屋兴宣、内阁参议池田成排、日本工业组合中央会长伍堂卓雄、日本商工会会议所所长八田嘉明。

A group photograph of Wang Yitang and Japanese high-ranking officials. Front Row, left to right: Ishiwata Shotaro, Yue Kaixian, Hirao Zenhachiro, Yuki Toyotaro, Morioka Toru, Wang Yitang, Go Seinosuke, Kaya Okinobu, Iketa Sebai, Godo Takuo and Yata Yoshiaki.

Officials of the puppet North China Provisional Government Wang Kemin, Wang Yitang, Qi Xieyuan, and Zhu Boyuan welcome Japanese scholars and experts to China in 1938.

1938年伪华北临时政府头目王克敏、王揖唐、齐燮元、朱伯渊欢迎永久等日本博士合影。

The Burmese delegation to China received a warm welcome in Kunming, December 12, 1939.

1939年12月12日缅甸访华团飞抵昆明时，受到中国政府欢迎，图为代表们在机场上谈话的情形。

People of Yunnan Province and the Burmese delegation, December 27, 1939.

1939年12月27日滇省各届人士欢送缅甸访华团返回缅甸时的合影。

Otani Nomizo, a Japanese scholar on *the Book of Changes*, visited Wang Yitang on Nov. 6, 1940. Right to left: Wang Runzhen, Wang Yitang, Otani Nomizo and Jin Siren.

1940年11月6日，日本易学家小谷吞象"拜访"王揖唐。右起王润贞、王揖唐、小谷吞象、荆嗣仁。

The Japanese special ambassador Takuma Taro, paid an official call on Wang Yitang who was chairman of the puppet North China Government Administrative Commission in 1941.

1941年，日本特命大使多熊太郎"拜谒"伪华北政务委员会委员长王揖唐。

The German ambassador paid a visit to the puppet North China Government Administrative Commission in June 1942. Here is the group photograph of the ambassador and Wang Yitang.

1942年6月德国驻华大使司达美访问伪华北政务委员会时，与王揖唐等人合影。

The German ambassador having a talk with Wang Yitang.

1942年6月德国驻华大使司达美访问伪华北政务委员会时与王揖唐会谈。

经济篇

ECONOMY

　　旧中国经济的增长非常缓慢,统一的全国市场从未组织起来,绝大多数中国人始终过着相当贫困的生活。

　　19世纪末叶,中国出现了弱小的近代工业和运输业,但是它们影响甚微。整个旧中国的经济是由一个庞大的农业部门和一个很小的非农业部门构成的。

　　本篇收集的照片的内容侧重于非农业部门,着重反映旧中国畸形的、半封建半殖民地的经济状况。内容主要包括以下几个方面:

　　旧中国的财政和金融:如清末政府户部设立的造币总厂、大清银行,民国时期的当铺等。

　　旧中国的商业:如各类综合或专业的市场,商业招牌和招幌,各类商业及服务业店铺,个体小商贩等。

　　旧中国的轻工业:如制瓷、晒盐、制毡、纺织等行业以及从事这些行业的各种手艺人。

　　旧中国的重工业:如列强在中国开办的矿业、旧中国政府兴办的矿业、军事工业等。

　　另外,本篇还收录了一些有关旧中国重大经济事件或活动,以及经济方面的政府机构、人物等照片。

　　Owing to the lack of a unified national economy, economic progress in Old China was slow and many of its people lived in poverty. By the end of the 19th century, modern industries and transportation were beginning to appear in China. They were, however, very weak and had little positive influence. The Chinese economy during this period was still largely dominated by an underdeveloped agricultural system. This chapter contains 60 photographs which illustrate the abnormal economic development brought by China's semi-colonial, and semi-feudal social experiences in such fields as finance, commerce and services, heavy and light industries.

　　Important business activities and related organs and personalities are also included in the Economy Chapter.

Guangdong Customs House, located in Haixian County, built in 1860 during the Second Opium War.

广东粤海关外景。此关于1860年第二次鸦片战争期间，由控制中国海关大权的英国人总税务司李泰国筹建，位于广东南海县城外。

In 1906, the Qing government refigured the Board of Revenue as the Ministry of Finance, which housed ten departments devoted to tax administration and the National Treasury. Here are officials of the new board.

1906年清朝政府改户部为度支部,内设田赋、漕仓、税课、库藏等十司,图为度支部库藏司官僚的合影。

In 1894, the Qing government, after suffering great pecuniary losses, stopped the production of copper coins. It was not until 1900, when Guangdong Province began using foreign-manufactured machines to produce the copper coins, that the venture became profitable. As a result, the Qing government ordered provinces in the coastal area to follow suit. Here is Jiangsu Copper Coin Bureau established in Feb. 1904.

1894年清朝政府鉴于铸制钱亏损甚巨,大钱又窒碍难行,下令停铸制钱。1900年广东首先用机器制造铜元,清朝政府从中获得利益,下令沿海各省仿广东之例开铸铜元。各省遂纷纷向外国采购机器,制造铜元。图为1904年2月建立的江苏铜元局正门全景。

The Mukden Incident (September 18, 1931) led to the Japanese occupation of Northeast China. In June 1932, the Central Bank of Manchuria, seen here, was founded.

"九•一八事变"后,日本占领中国东北,于1932年3月宣布设立伪"满洲中央银行"。同年6月伪"满洲中央银行"正式成立。图为"满洲中央银行"外景。

In May 1930, the Tihwah Sino-American Business Firm went into operation in what is now the city of Urumchi.

1930年5月迪化(今新疆乌鲁木齐)华美洋行开业照片。

1904 saw the establishment of the first modern national bank in China. In 1908, the bank was renamed the Bank of Qing with its headquarters in Beijing. Soon branches were established all over the country. Here is the Bank of Qing, Harbin Branch, which was opened in August 1910.

1904年中国第一个近代性质的国家银行——清朝户部银行成立,1908年改称大清银行。该行总行设在北京,陆续在各地建立分行。图为1910年8月大清银行哈尔滨分行开办时的全景。

The Financial Department of Guangdong Province in the early republican era.

民国初年的广东财政厅外景

In order to mitigate corruption, the Qing government took over the right of coinage from local governments and set up the General Mint in Tianjin on Aug. 22, 1905. It was under the control of the Board of Revenue. Here are officials from the Board of Revenue and the General Mint.

1905年8月22日，清朝政府为了消除各省制造铜元的流弊，收回制造权，于天津成立户部造币总厂，统一制造。图为开办户部造币总厂的户部官员和造币总厂官员合影。

The General Mint under the control of the Board of Revenue, Aug. 1905.

1905年8月户部造币总厂外景。

Hubei Hanyang Copper Mill, built in the late years of the Qing Dynasty, was one of the subsidiaries of Hubei Gun Factory, which was planned and sponsored by Zhang Zhidong. The copper mill primarily produced bullets and artillery shells.

湖北汉阳炼铜厂是与清末张之洞筹办的湖北枪炮厂相配套的军事工业之一，主要制造各类枪炮子弹。

Hubei Hanyang Arsenal, established in 1892 by Zhang Zhidong, governor of Hukwang, produced guns and artilleries.

湖北汉阳兵工厂是1892年由清湖广总督张之洞筹办的，制造各种枪炮，是清朝政府兴办的重要的近代军事工业之一。

Fushun Coal Mine was exploited by the Japanese following the Russo-Japanese War. Here is Fushun Coal Mine in the early republican era.

抚顺煤矿。1907年日俄战争之后，日本从清朝政府手中接管了抚顺煤矿，划归南伪满洲铁道株式会社管理，成为日本在华工业投资、掠夺中国矿业资源的项目之一。这是民国初期抚顺煤矿的采掘情况。

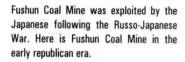

Hubei Daye Iron Mine, an official enterprise, was established by Sheng Xuanhuai during the late years of the Qing Dynasty. After 1899, it was largely funded with Japanese capital.

湖北大冶铁矿是清末由盛宣怀主持兴办的官营近代矿业之一。1899年之后逐步为日本资本所控制。图为该矿采掘实况。

The power plant at the Tianfu Coal Mine, 1943.

1943年天府煤矿的电厂发电机

A timber mill in Northeast China run by Japanese during the Manchukuo period.

伪满时期日本人在中国东北开的木材厂

A tin mill in the ore-rich Yunnan Province in the early republican era.

云南个旧地区盛产锡矿。图为民国初年云南省锡的洗矿和制炼情形。

A porcelain kiln in Cizhou, Hebei,
post 1911.

民国时期河北磁州的窑场远景

Windmills at a salt mine.　盐田潮汐水风车

Yingkou Salt Mine, circa 1930.

民国时期的营口盐田

A porcelain workshop in Jiujiang, during the republican period.

民国时期江西九江制瓷业

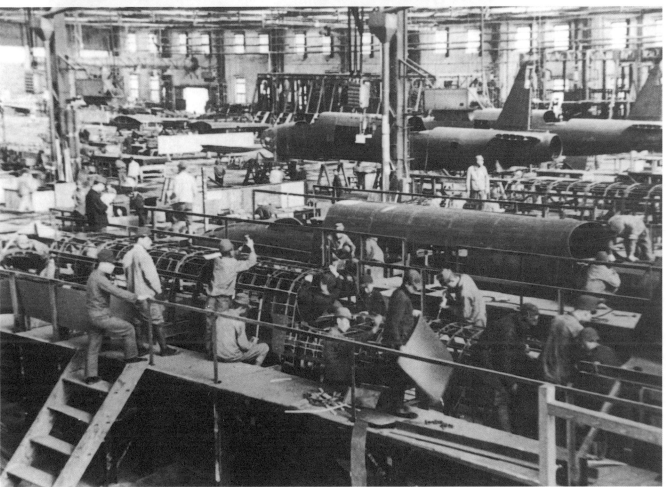

After the start of the Sino-Japanese War, Japan established a number of military enterprises in the puppet state of Manchukuo to support her war machine. Here is a Japanese aircraft factory in Manchukuo.

1937年"七·七事变"后，日本为了扩大战争的需要，妄图将中国东北变成其军事装备的生产基地，在伪满洲国建立了一系列军事工业。图为日本在伪满建立的航空军事工业——伪满洲飞机工厂。

In 1874, Lu Runxiang established the Sulun Spinning Bureau in Suzhou, which was equipped with western-style looms.

1874年苏州商务局陆润庠筹建位于苏州的苏纶纺纱局，采用西方近代纺纱技术。图为该厂机器抽花条的情形。

In 1897, Lu Runxiang established Jiangsu Sujing Spinning Mill in Suzhou.

1897年由商务局陆润庠筹建位于苏州的江苏苏经缫丝厂。图为该厂女工在缫丝。

A silkworm nursery tended by aboriginal inhabitants of Taiwan in 1940, while under the colonial rule of Japan.

1940年日殖时期台湾土著居民养蚕蚕房。图为给蚕喂桑叶的情形。

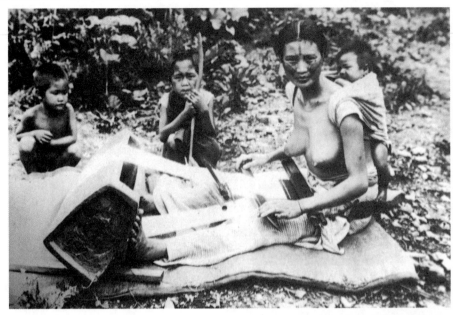

A Taiwanese woman weaving cloth during the island's colonial period.

日殖时期台湾当地妇女手工机织土布的情形

Mongolian women making felt by hand, during the republican period.

在蒙古牧区，手工制毡是传统手工业之一。图为民国时期阿巴嘎王府一带蒙古族妇女手工缝制毛毡的情形。

Wool spinning is a traditional handicraft industry of Inner Mongolia. Here craftsmen in Baotou spinning wool during the republican era.

纺羊毛是内蒙古一带的传统手工业之一。图为民国时期包头工匠纺织羊毛的情形。

During the first and second decades of the twentieth century, peddlers wandered from place to place selling daily necessities. They often beat a small drum to attract customers.

清末民初在城乡中走街串巷的小商贩,他们挑着货担,内装各种与百姓日常生活有关的小商品、小食品,并用各种方法,如:吆喝、摇小货郎鼓等招引人注意。

An oil peddler in the early republican period.

民国初年推独轮车卖油者

Workers towing a wooden boat against the mighty current of the Yangtze River.

依靠人力、风力的旧木船,在长江、黄河等湍急的大河中逆流而上,都须用纤夫拉纤,他们唱着古老的号子,迈着沉重的步伐,一步步牵引着船上行。图为长江上纤夫拉纤的情形。

Using a small furnace, blacksmiths make and repair farm tools, pots and pans, and other utensils. This picture was taken in Liaoning Province during the 1930's.

路旁的铁匠炉是依靠小火炉手工制造修理小型农具等生产、生活用具。图为民国时期辽宁开原路旁，铁匠炉锻造的情形。

A porridge stand in the early republican period. 民国初年街头粥摊

A Tea stand on Taishan Mountain, Shandong Province.

民国时期泰山上卖茶水的小摊

In old times, barbers, carrying stands on their backs, went from place to place to shave their customers. Here is a barber with his stand which contains a small stove, a bronze basin and a tool box.

旧时剃头匠挑着一边是放理发工具的小柜、一边是小火炉的剃头挑子,在街头巷尾为主顾剃头、刮脸。图为剃头匠正在用剃刀为顾客剃头,旁边的小火炉上放置铜盆、热水,用于给顾客洗头。

In republican period, the Li People inhabited Hainan Island, where they supported themselves by fishing.

民国时期海南岛黎族男子,他们肩负渔网,臂挎渔篓,在捕鱼途中。

A whaling boat, 1929.

1929年的捕鲸船。

In China's frigid northern regions, large blocks of ice were cut from frozen rivers and lakes and stored in ice cellars, where it stayed until it was needed during the summer.

旧时冬季，北方各地都有将自然冰块取出窖藏的职业，以备夏季使用。图为拉冰块者正在运输采取的冰块。

Farmers, living in Taichung, Taiwan, transport sugar canes with buffalo carts during the Japanese colonial period.

日殖时期，台湾台中农民用水牛运输甘蔗的情形。

Zhangjiakou was well renowned for its prosperous leather and fur trade.

张家口地区是关外皮货进入关内的重要集散地。街道上众多的皮货摊，反映了张家口皮货贸易的兴隆景象。

Herbs used for medicinal purposes were dried in this way in Nanchang during the republican period.

民国时期南昌手工药房晒制草药。

The Guangsheng Drug Store in republican period, sold both Chinese and Western medicines.

广生药房及伙计。该药房是一个民国时期中西药兼备的成药房。

In the old days, paper articles such as paper soldiers, paper horses and paper money were burned as offerings to the dead at funerals. Here is a special market selling such goods in the republican period.

冥市。旧时为死人丧葬祭典，都要烧陪葬的纸人纸马纸钱等阴间冥物。图为民国时期集市中专卖冥物的市场。

A bird shop in Shanghai in the republican era which specialized in exquisite cages and exotic birds.

民国时期上海卖鸟的小店。方的、圆的各种各样的鸟笼内，关着各种漂亮、鸣叫声悦耳的观赏鸟，卖给爱好养鸟者消遣。

Farmers in Nanjing, Jiangsu, used such water wheel to irrigate their field during the republican period.

民国时期江苏南京一带用脚踏水车灌溉水田的情形

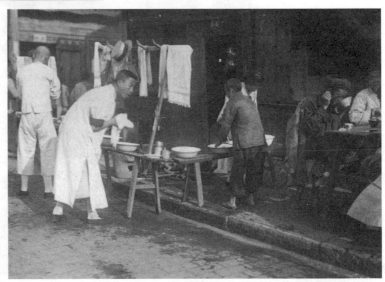

A wash room, Kunming, Yunnan.

云南省昆明夏季的洗脸屋

A fireworks shop, Beijing. 北京卖爆竹的商店

A blacksmith changing a donkey's iron shoes. This photograph was taken in Shanhaiguan Pass, during the early republican period.

民国初年山海关街旁马掌铺。图为匠人正在给驴换掌的情形。

A jewelry shop.

经营金银首饰及工艺品的商店

Baoluyuan Goldsmith's Shop traded in gold and silver jewelry as well as raw gold.

装饰华丽的大黑河宝陆源金店。专卖各类金银首饰器皿，并收购砂金。

A second-hand bookstore in the early republican period. Every book in the store is tagged with its name and price.

民国初年的旧书店。每部书都夹有纸条，上书书名、标价，使顾客一目了然。

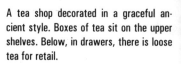

A tea shop decorated in a graceful ancient style. Boxes of tea sit on the upper shelves. Below, in drawers, there is loose tea for retail.

饮茶是中华民族古老而广泛的嗜好之一。图为一间装饰漂亮的茶叶店。柜厨上有筒装、盒装的各种茶叶销售，下面的抽屉里则是各种散装零售的茶叶。

In old times, many restaurants had private dining rooms. This photograph shows a waiter in a Beijing restaurant, carrying three bronze Mongolian hot pots on his shoulder to a gracefully decorated private room.

旧时比较讲究的饭馆，既有散座、也有雅座。图为北京某饭馆设在楼上的单间雅座，内有衣帽架、壁饰、字画等，环境幽雅。店内跑堂肩托木盘，上有紫铜火锅三个。

There are thousands of tea houses in China, but the most famous are in Sichuan Province. Here is a large formal tea house, where people drink tea, chat, entertain themselves and conduct business.

1929年的一座茶馆。茶馆遍布华夏大地，以四川最盛。这是一座规模较大而正规的茶馆。茶馆不仅是品茗饮茶的地方，也是人们消遣、做买卖、谈生意的聚集地。

An open-air market in Dalian City during the republican period. It sells various articles including groceries, second-hand goods and daily necessities.

民国时期的大连露天市场,买卖各种杂货、旧货及日用品等物。

A tobacco shop selling cut tobacco, flue-cured tobacco and other smoking products.

烟草铺,从货架上可见各类烟丝、烤烟叶等。

The timber market in Shuangchahe, Jilin. This market was very large during the republican period. At that time, timber was transported by sleds.

中国东北三省盛产木材。图为民国时期吉林双岔河的木材市场。买卖木材者用爬犁将木材、圆材运到市场交易。从画面看这个木材市场颇具规模。

A Chinese cabbage market in Shandong Province during the republican period. Cabbage produced in Shandong is very large, weighing from 5 to 10 kilograms each.

民国时期山东某地的白菜市场。图中的白菜为山东特产，棵大，每棵重在5——10公斤，菜质细嫩，为北方冬季的最佳贮藏蔬菜。

A produce shop in Guangdong, in the republican period.

民国时期广州市内的水果店铺，各式水果异常丰盛鲜亮。

Guangshenlong Warehouse located on the outskirts of Beijing, and its billboards.

北京郊外带有广告牌的广盛隆货栈门面

In the republican period, nearly every shop had a special sign to solicit customers. Here is a street lined with various gaily-painted stores.

民国时期沿街店面的商店招幌。从图面上看,这条街道,摊店彼此相连,招幌令人眼花缭乱。

Shop signs during the period of Japanese occupation.

日伪时期商店的招牌

The simple sign of a grocery store in a small village.

乡间杂货小卖部的招牌

Even after a modern banking system was introduced in China, pawnbroking, persisted as a traditional method of loaning money.

典当业是中国古老而传统的一种高利信贷行业。在近代银行业兴起之后，这种行业仍然存在。图为装饰非常派场的当铺招牌。

The high counter of a pawnshop.　　安装铁栅栏的当铺柜台

Duoyuan Pawnshop in Heilongjiang Province in the republican period.

民国时期黑龙江某地的多源当铺门面。

交通篇 TRAFFIC & COMMUNICATIONS

俗话说:"要想富,先修路。"交通直接影响着国民经济的盛衰。而极不发达的交通运输恰恰一直是旧中国经济的主要弱点之一。

曾几何时,泱泱中华繁荣的水陆交通网举世瞩目,但随着社会的日益发展,陈旧缓慢的木船和人畜力车也日益落后于时代,已不能承载经济命脉这副重担。

19世纪中叶,锁国的大门被打开,西方列强为了加强政治和经济侵略,开始出资兴建铁路、港口,他们在中国开办的轮船公司、铁路公司给中国传统的交通运输业以巨大冲击。另一方面,清末朝廷里的"自强派"以及后来的军阀、国民党政府,出于经济和战略方面的考虑,也修建了一些铁路和码头。但是,需要指出的是:这些交通设施的建设没有统一的规划,而且数量有限,分布不均,运营效率极低。在广大的中国农村及部分内陆城镇,仍依赖于古老的驿路、运河交通运输。

本篇这组历史照片着重反映旧中国的中外航运、铁路、公路的建设情况,诸如海运的塘沽、大连,内河的哈尔滨、汉口等航运码头;京奉线、津浦线、正太线、粤汉线、东省铁路、川省铁路等铁路;另外,我们还收录了一些与这些交通设备有关的照片,如铁路工厂、车站码头的货场栈房、机车轮船的运行情况,以及一些重大的有关交通的会议、事件、人物。

A Chinese saying asserts, "Where there is a road, there is sure to be prosperity." It is undeniable that communication plays a vital role in the development of a national economy. The prevailing poverty in nineteenth century China was largely due to the lack of easy and efficient transportation.

In ancient times, China's transportation network was quite advanced relative to other nations. However, as time passed on, ancient wooden boats and animal-drawn carts could no longer meet the needs of modern industry.

During the mid-19th century, China was forced to open its door to the outside world. Soon Western powers began building railroads and ports in an effort to exploit China's natural resources and broaden their spheres of influence. The Western methods of transportation forced the ancient Chinese methods into obsolescence. The Qing Dynasty, the post-1911 warlords, and the Kuomintang government built a number of railways and ports in an attempt to meet the needs of the economy and to aid in national defense. These limited transportation facilities, however, neither had the uniform planning, nor the technical efficiency needed to make them profitable. In most rural areas and in some landlocked cities, ancient post roads and canals were still crucial to transportation.

Hulin Port, Heilongjiang Province, in the early republican period.

民国初年的黑龙江省虎林码头

Wharves on the Haihe River, Tianjin, in the early republican period.

民国初年间天津海河上的码头

A 3,000-tonnage dock at the Tanggu New Port, built in the early republican period.

民国初年修建中的塘沽新港三千吨级船坞

Guanlun Port, Jilin, toward the end of the Qing Dynasty.

清朝末年的吉林官轮码头

After Shanghai was forced to open to the outside world in 1842, Western powers began to build wharves in an effort to exploit China's natural recourses and dump their products. Here is a Japanese mail boat dock in Shanghai, 1919.

1842年上海开埠后，西方列强掠夺中国资源，倾销商品，相继在上海建造各国的码头。图为1919年的上海日本邮船码头全景。

The Ningbo Port, Zhejiang, in the early days of the republican era.　民国初年的浙江宁波码头

Hankou Port, 1909.
1909年的汉口码头

The New Hankou Port in the early days of the republican era.
民国初年的新汉口码头

Jiujiang Port.
民国初年的九江码头

Xiaguan Port, Nanjing, Jiangsu, in the early republican period. This port was constructed in 1882.

民国初年的南京下关码头。该码头于1882年由轮船招商局始建。

Shashi Port, Hubei, 1909.　　1909年的湖北沙市码头

Kaohsiung Port, Taiwan, while
under the Japanese colonization.
日殖时期的台湾高雄港

Keelung Port, Taiwan, while
under Japanese control.
日殖时期的台湾基隆港

A section of the ancient Grand Canal
in Suzhou during the 1900's.
清末苏州一带的古大运河

民国时期的广州运河
The Guangzhou Canal during
the republican period.

The inland water transport
conditions in Tianjin City toward
the end of the Qing Dynasty.

清朝末年的天津内河运输

Gong'an Street, Beijing, during
the republican era.

民国时期的北京公安街

The railroad from Majiabao to Zhengyang-men, Beijing. A section of the Jingfeng Railway was built by a British company in 1901. Here is the Qianmen Railway Station, Beijing, still under construction.

1901年英国人修筑京奉铁路马家堡至北京正阳门一段。图为正在修建中的北京前门火车站。

A post road in the Zhuozi Mountain area, post 1911.

民国初年卓资山的驿路

The railroad from Majiabao to Zhengyang-men, Beijing. A section of the Jingfeng Railway, the first railway to Beijing, was complete in 1901. This picture shows a train passing through Rademen (present Chongwenmen).

1901年京奉铁路北京——马家堡段完工。图为进入北京的第一条铁路(京奉铁路)通过哈德门(今崇文门)的情景。

Between 1874 and 1876, the British and American Wusong Road Company built a railroad running 14.5 kilometers from Wusong to Shanghai. The railroad was removed after control of it was regained by the Qing government. Here is a section of the railroad.

1874—1876年英美"吴淞道路公司"修建吴淞到上海全长14.5公里的铁路线。1877年由清朝政府赎回后拆毁。图为原上海淞沪铁路的一段。

During the Russo-Japanese War (1904—1905), Japan built this light narrow-gauge railway from Xinmin County to Mukden (present Shenyang), as a section of the Jingfeng Railway. It was rebuilt into a standard-gauge railway when it was reclaimed by the Qing government. Here is the railroad while still under Japanese control.

1904—1905年日俄战争期间，由日本修筑的京奉铁路，新民府至奉天（今沈阳）为窄轨轻便铁路。1907年由清政府赎回，改成标准轨。此图为尚未改为标准轨时的情形。

In accordance with the Sino-Russian Secret Treaty, Russia, in 1896, started to build the Dongsheng Railway (also called the Dongqing or Zhongdong Railway) running from Manzhouli to Suifenhe. The railway was constructed and administrated by the Russia Dongsheng Railway Company, shown here.

1896年沙俄根据《中俄密约》规定，在中国东北修筑由满洲里到绥芬河的东省铁路（又称东清铁路、中东铁路），1898年至1903年修筑完工通车。该路由沙俄的东省铁路公司管理修筑、运营。图为东省铁路公司外景。

American and Russian locomotives and box cars running on the Dongsheng Railway toward the end of the Qing Dynasty.
清末在东省铁路上运行的美式、俄式机车及货车。

Between 1898 and 1903, Russia built the Dongsheng Railway, which began construction in Harbin City. Tracks were laid eastward to Suifenhe and westward to Manzhouli respectively. Here is the eastern platform of Harbin Station.
1898—1903年沙俄以哈尔滨为中心，东向绥芬河、西向满洲里，分段修筑东省铁路。图为东省铁路哈尔滨车站及东站月台全景。

清末东省铁路上运行的货车车箱 Box cars running on the Dongsheng Railway.

The ticket office at Tanggu Station on the Jingfeng Railway during the 1900's.
清末修筑的京奉铁路塘沽车站票房

Between 1905 and 1909, Zhan Tianyou was commissioned as chief engineer by the Qing Government to build the Jing-zhang Railway. Here are locomotive houses at Nankou.

1905—1909年清朝政府任命詹天佑为总工程师,修筑北京——张家口铁路(京张线)。图为京张线的南口机车房。

Tracks at Qinglongqiao along the Jing-zhang Railway were laid in a 'Z' forma-tion to negotiate steep slopes. Chief Engineer Zhan Tianyou was responsible for this remarkable design.

图为清末修筑的京张线青龙桥的"之"型铁路,上下铁路正同时开行,它是詹天佑设计的京张线中具有代表性的杰作。

A water tower and its well house in Shaziling, on the Jingzhang Railway.

清末修筑的京张线沙岭子水塔及井房

A locomotive house on the Jingzhang Railway.

清末修筑的京张线上的停车场房

In order to build the Jingfeng Railroad, the Qing government founded the Shanhaiguan Bridge Construction Plant. Here are pipe driving machines in the plant.

清末为修筑京奉路开设的山海关造桥厂打桩架

To aid in the construction of the Jingfeng Railroad, the Qing government founded the Shanhaiguan Railway Engineering Plant.

清末为修筑京奉路开设的山海关铁路工程厂

From 1909 to 1922, the Chinese government extended the Jingzhang Railway to Baoto. Thus the Jingsui Railway (Beijing to Suiyuan) came into being. This photo shows the Dayang River Bridge, connecting Zhangjiakou and Gaoyang, being built in 1911.

1909—1922年，中国政府延长京张线至包头，形成京绥线。图为京绥线张家口至高阳段的大洋河桥1911年正在施工的情形。

The Shanhaiguan Railroad Bridge on the Jingfeng Railway, built toward the end of the Qing Dynasty.

清末修筑在京奉线上的山海关铁道桥

The Liaohe Railroad Bridge constructed in 1907. It connects Xinmin County and Mukden (present Shenyang), which is a section of the Jingfeng Railway.

1907年间修筑京奉线新民府至奉天(今沈阳)铁路段的辽河铁桥施工情形

The De'an Railroad Bridge on the Nanxun Railway, which was built between 1908 and 1916 running from Nanchang to Jiujiang, Jiangxi Province.

1908—1916年中国政府修筑了江西南昌至九江的南浔铁路。图为南浔铁路德安铁路大桥。

The 200-*chi*-long railroad bridge on the Huhang Railway (Shanghai to Hangzhou), built between 1906 and 1909.

1906—1909年修筑上海至杭州的沪杭铁路。图为该路斜塘上二百尺双空二十尺双环桥。

A stone arch bridge on the highway from Chengdu to Chongqing.

成都至重庆公路上的石拱桥

念紀站開步遙德英路粵日五廿月一年二國民

In January 1913, Yaobu Station on the Yuehan Railway (Guangdong to Hankou) was opened to traffic.

1913年1月，粵汉路英德遥步开站纪念。

Langfang Station on the Jingfeng Railway, completed in 1894.

1894年建成的京奉铁路廊坊车站

Between 1898 and 1903, Russia built the Binzhou Section of the Dongsheng Railway in Northeast China. Manzhouli Station is shown here.

1898—1903年沙俄在中国东北修筑的东省铁路滨洲段满洲里车站

The Yuehan Railway was constructed between 1906 and 1936. The Guangdong Section was run by a business group. Here is Huangsha (Guangdong) Station, completed in 1912.

1906—1936年修筑了武昌至广州的粤汉铁路,其中广东段为商办。图为1912年修建完成的粤汉铁路黄沙(即广州)车站。

Russia built the Dongsheng Railway between 1889 and 1903. Below are Ajihei and Tsitsihar stations on the Binzhou Section.

1898—1903年沙俄在中国修筑的东省铁路,图为滨州段上齐齐哈尔、阿什河车站月台和外景。

Between 1922 and 1924, warlords of Northeast China signed a treaty with Japan to built the Yanji Railway. Here is the newly completed Yanji Station.

1922—1924年由中国东北军阀与日本协定,中日官商合办延吉铁路线。图为新建成的延吉火车站。

Hsiahuayuan Station on the Jingzhang Railway was completed in 1909.

1909年清朝政府修建完成的京张线下花园车站

The Jingzhang Railway, built by the Qing government, was opened to traffic on Oct. 2, 1909.

1909年10月2日清朝政府修筑的京张铁路通车典礼上，南口茶会专列入站情景。

Chingho (Qinghe) Station on the Jingzhang Railway was completed in 1909.

1909年清朝政府修建完成的京张线清河车站

The Qing government built the Jinpu Railway (Tianjin to Pukou) between 1908 and 1911. Here is the newly completed Pukou Station.

1908—1911年清朝政府借款修筑了天津至浦口的津浦铁路。图为新修建成的津浦路浦口车站。

The Guang'anmen Station on the Jingzhang Railway built in 1909.

1909年由清朝政府修建的京张线广安门车站

Between 1907 and 1908, the Qing government added a branch line to the Jingzhang Railway, running from Xizhimen to Mentougou, Beijing. The Mentougou Station is shown here.

1907—1908年清朝政府修筑的京张铁路北京西直门——门头沟支线上的门头沟车站

Between 1908 and 1916, the Nanxun Railway from Nanchang to Jiujiang was built. Here is the newly completed Jiujiang Station.

1908—1916年修建南昌至九江的南浔铁路。图为新修建成的九江火车站。

By the help of foreign loans, the Qing government laid tracks between Shijiazhuang and Taiyuan from 1904 — 1907. According to the original plan, the railway would begin at Zhengding. Later the starting point was changed to Taiyuan, but the name of the railway, "Zhengtai", remained. This group photo of foreign experts and engineers was taken in October 1907, when the Zhengtai Railway was opened to traffic.

1904—1907年清朝政府向外国借款修筑由石家庄至太原(原计划由正定至太原, 后改为由石家庄至太原, 故原称正太路名称未改)。图为1907年10月正太铁路通车时外国专家与工程人员的合影。

A stone arch bridge on the Zhengtai Railway.

1904—1907年修筑的正太铁路石拱桥之一

Railroad engineers during the 1900's — standing in the middle is Zhan Tianyou.

清末詹天佑(中立者)等铁路工程设计人员合影

The Chinese Engineering Society was founded in February 1912. Here are the participants of its first conference.

1912年2月在广州成立的中华工程司学会第一次会议代表合影。

A tunnel on the Zhengtai Railway.

1904—1907年修筑的正太铁路隧洞之一

Zhan Tianyou (first from right) and his colleagues in 1905 — 1909, while building the Jingzhang Railway.

1905—1909年詹天佑(右一)主持修筑京张铁路时与同僚合影。

Zhan Tianyou was commissioned by the Qing government during the 1900's to supervise construction of the Yuehan Railway. Here is a group photograph of the General Federation of the Yuehan Railway. Front row, seventh from left, is Zhan Tianyou.

清末清朝政府任命詹天佑为粤汉铁路督办。图为民国初年詹天佑(前排左七)等在粤汉铁路总会前合影。

The Guangdong Yuehan Railway Business Company chose Zhan Tianyou to act as general manager and chief engineer in 1910. Here, Zhan Tianyou inspects the Yingde Bridge on the Yuehan Railway in 1910 after arriving in Guangdong. Standing in the middle is Kuang Sunmou, to his left is Zhan Tianyou.

1910年商办广东粤汉铁路公司推举詹天佑任总理兼总工程师,于是,清朝政府将已到宜昌川汉铁路公司的詹天佑调任粤汉铁路督办。图为1910年后詹天佑到广东,视察粤汉路英德大桥。中立者为邝孙谋,左为詹天佑。

The Chuanhan Railway Company, Sichuan Province, was founded in 1907. After completion of the Jingzhang Railway in 1909, Zhan Tianyou and Yan Deqing were commissioned by the Qing government as chief and vice-chief engineers of the Chuanhan Railway. In December of the same year, a section of the railway from Yichang to Wanxian was started, but later aborted. Here is a group photograph taken to commemorate the start of construction on the Chuanhan Railway. Standing in the middle, left is Zhan Tianyou and right is Li Jixun.

1907年四川省川汉铁路公司成立。1909年京张铁路完工后，清朝政府调詹天佑、颜德庆分别为川汉路正副总工程师。同年12月川汉路宜昌至万县段开工。此路后停工废弃。此图为川汉铁路在宜昌举行开工典礼时各届人士的合影。中间三人左为詹天佑，右为李稷勋。

After handed over his position to Yuan Shikai on April 1, 1912, Dr. Sun Yet-sen declared his dedication to the industrial development of China. This group photograph was taken on May 17, 1912, when the Guangdong Yuehan Railway Business Company held a welcoming party for Dr. Sun Yet-sen, seated in the middle. First from right is Zhan Tianyou.

1912年4月1日孙中山先生宣布解除临时总统职，将权利移交给袁世凯，声称在野发展实业。此图为1912年5月17日商办粤路公司欢迎孙中山先生时合影。右一为詹天佑，右三为孙中山。

赈灾篇

DISASTER RELIEF

水、旱、虫等自然灾害自古以来就是人类生存的大敌,人类始终与它们进行着不懈的斗争,在求得自身生存和繁衍的同时,也不断地改造着大自然。中华民族就是在这种与大自然的顽强斗争中,一步步成熟、兴盛起来,并且在改造自然环境方面创造了辉煌的业绩。

中华民族赖以生存的神州大地素有南涝北旱之害,黄河、长江、淮河等大江大河哺育了炎黄子孙,但他们同时又是民族生存的大患。在旧中国,清政府的昏聩无能、民国初年的长期政治分裂与军阀混战,人为地削弱了中华民族抵御自然灾害的能力,致使全国各地水灾、旱灾、虫灾连绵不断,处处灾害横行,哀鸿遍野,一片凄惨景象。

本篇精选五十余幅照片,首先集中展示了旧中国的一些重大灾情,如民国初年天津海河泛滥、拒马河水淹没涿州;察哈尔的连年大旱、陕西的大旱;1935年黄河决口、江汉湘数处空前的大水灾等等;其次反映了这些灾害过后政府的一些赈济、安抚灾民的举动,包括清政府、民国政府以及受民国政府委托的华洋义赈会举办的一些赈灾活动;另外,本篇还收录了与抗灾有关的水利工程的照片,如海河清淤工程、旧黄河水利委员会主持修固的黄河大堤、陕西水利局针对1929年大旱开凿的泾惠渠,等等。

Natural disasters such as floods, draughts and insects, have plagued mankind throughout history. While fighting against these disasters, man also learned to improve living conditions. The Chinese people matured and grew stronger in the face of such natural disasters.

China does not enjoy favorable natural conditions. The South is often stricken by floods, while the North suffers from severe draught. The Yellow and Yangtze rivers flooded frequently but irregularly in ancient times, devastating the people and the great civilization they worked to develop. Due to the poor management of the Qing government and the long term civil warfare among warlords, old China was constantly inundated with disaster-stricken refugees.

In this chapter, 50 selected photographs reveal for the first time a few of the most serious disasters such as the Haihe River flood in Tianjin 1917, the Juma River flood in Zhuozhou, the lasting draughts in Chahar and Shanxi provinces, the Yellow River flood in 1935 and the floods along the middle reaches of the Yangtze River. Special attention is also paid to the measures taken by the Qing and the Republican governments to provide relief to the afflicted areas. In addition, related water conservation projects, whose aim was to prevent such disasters in the future are included in this chapter.

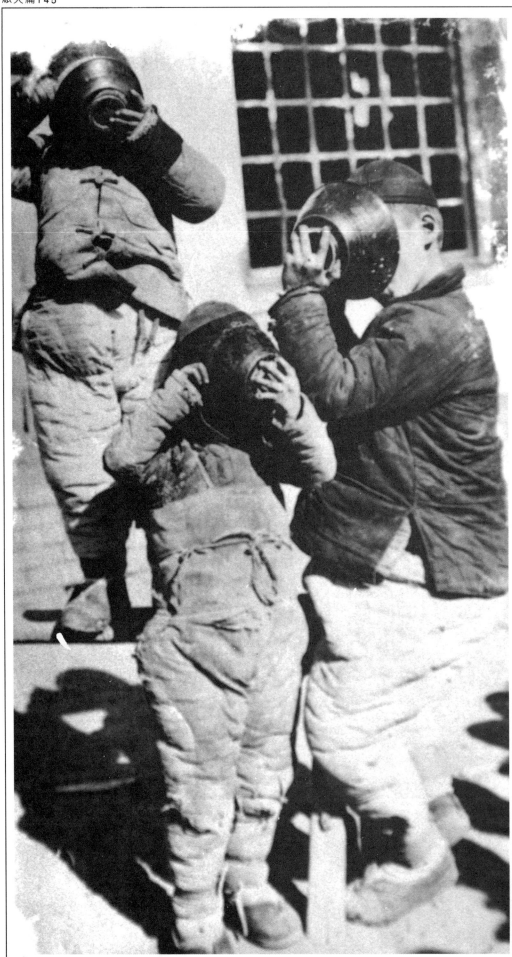

Hungry children in Beijing eating gruel at a relief kitchen in the early republican era.

民国初年北京施粥厂三儿童食粥的情形。

The Dasha River overflowed its banks in Xinle County in 1924. The flood destroyed a section of the Jinghan Railway.

1924年大沙河在河北省新乐县的决口处。此次大水冲毁了京汉铁路。

A serious flood plagued Hebei and Shandong provinces in July 1917. Statistics show that the flood destroyed 103 counties and 6.35 million people lost their homes. Here is a flooded street in the town of Zhuozhou near the Juma River.

1917年7月冀鲁地区发生特大水灾,以河北省灾情最重,据统计,被淹103个县,灾民达635万人。图为拒马河水泛滥,淹没涿州城街道的情形。

The Haihe River flooded Tianjin City in July 1917 leaving 100,000 people homeless. Local garrison, the No. 2 Regiment of No. 1 Composite Brigade of the Beiyang Army, was dispatched to reinforce the dikes.

1917年7月天津海河发大水后,洪水淹没天津城,十万人无家可归。图为驻天津北洋第一混成旅第二团赴工地情形。

People seeking refuge from the floods in make-shift shelters at Beiyingmen, on either side of the Jinpu Railway, Tianjin, 1917.

1917年天津大水后,灾民避水在北营门津浦路席棚内暂栖。

The Qinglong Temple, inside the barracks of the No. 5 Branch Garrison doubled as a refugee camp.

1917年天津大水后,天津中区第五分驻所界内青龙庙外也成为灾民的安身之地。

A lasting drought struck Shaanxi, Gansu, Shanxi and Chahar provinces between 1925 and 1929. About 34 million people suffered from the drought and many of them were compelled to leave their homes. Here is a depopulated village in the Manshou Mountain area, Changbao County, Chahar.

1925—1929年陕甘晋察连续大旱,灾民达3400万,赤地千里,种植维艰,难民流落异乡。图为察哈尔省昌宝县馒首山村人迹全无的惨状。

The Yellow River overflowed the No. 2 Xunbao Dam, Kaifeng, in August 1934.

1934年8月黄河洪水冲塌开封汛堡二坝的情形。

The Yellow River flooded at Huoxian County, Shanxi, on August 25, 1935.

1935年8月25日，黄河洪水从山西省霍县奔流直下的情形。

The Yellow River flooded many villages in Dongming County, Shandong on July 14, 1935.

1935年7月14日，黄河涨水冲塌山东省东明县一带房屋。

The Yellow River overflowed at Dong-zhuang Village, Juanxian County, Shandong, in July 1935. This photo of the flood is an example of early Chinese aerial photography.

1935年7月,黄河在山东省鄄县董庄决口。图为我国首次运用航拍技术拍摄的决口情形。

The Yellow River overflowed in Juanxian and Putai counties in July 1935. The flood also affected the nearby Heze, Yuncheng, and Jiaxiang counties. Above right is the south gate of Jiaxiang County surrounded by the flood. Right is a flooded street in the town of Yanshikou.

1935年7月黄河在鄄县、蒲台决口,水浸菏泽、郓城、嘉祥县等,由运河入江苏。以上两图为山东省嘉祥县南门被淹情形,闫什口镇的大街也变成黄河水道。

The flood along the middle reaches of the Yangtze River wiped out many houses in Lixian County, Hunan, July 1935.

1935年7月，长江中游大水，湖南省澧县津市房舍被冲毁。

Huarong County devastated by the flood in 1935.

1935年华容大水淹没农庄房舍情景。

Dikes in Huarong County, Hunan, were destroyed by the Yangtze River in July 1935.

1935年7月，长江中游大水，图为湖南省华容县第四区堤圩溃口的情形。

The flood left nothing but ruin in Ningxiang County, Hunan, July 1935.

1935年7月,长江中游大水,湖南省宁乡县被水淹后的惨景。

Victims of the flood, Ruanling County, Hunan, July 1935.

1935年7月,长江中游大水,湖南省沅陵县第二区的灾民。

The Wushui River in Jiangxi Province flooded on August 3, 1935. Farmers of Laoguanzui Village, Xinjian County, had to take refuge in make-shift shelters upland.

1935年8月3日,江西省婺水泛滥,新建县老观咀农民为避水灾搭在高地的茅舍。

Hengyang County, Hunan, surrounded by
water, July 1935.

1935年7月,长江中游大水,湖南省
衡阳县被水淹浸的惨状。

The Yellow River engulfed Yanshi City in 1935. 1935年黄河泛滥,河南省偃师市
被水淹的惨状。

The flood-stricken Hanchuan County, Hubei, July 1935.

1935年7月,长江中游大水,湖北省汉川县被水淹的惨景。

Wangcheng Village was destroyed when the Ziya River in Qingxian County, Hebei, flooded in 1946.

1946年河北省青县子牙河泛滥,王程庄被水淹浸。

Drinking water could only be drawn from wells in the southwestern part of Xi'an City, Shaanxi. The picture was taken during the republican period.

陕西省西安城内的井水,唯城西南角井水为甜水,可供食用。图为民国年间西安城内甜水井的某汲水井。

Jueluoxue Relief Kitchen, Beijing, 1910.
1910年的北京觉罗学粥厂

Guandimiao Relief Kitchen, Beijing, toward the end of the Qing Dynasty.
清末北京关帝庙粥厂

Fuleyuan Relief Kitchen, Beijing, during the 1900's.
清末北京福乐园粥厂

Xinfayuan Relief Kitchen, Beijing, in the late Qing Dynasty.

清末北京新发园粥厂

The Juma River in Zhuoxian County, Hebei, flooded in 1917. The local government sent officials to supervise the cooking of mantou (steamed bread) in a relief station.

1917年河北省涿县拒马河水泛滥后,临时赈济所监视蒸馒头。

Flood refugees receiving food, Zhuoxian County, Hebei, 1917.

1917年河北省涿县拒马河洪水后,各乡灾民到赈济所领干粮。

Policemen distributing mantou to refugees in front of the Li Hongzhang's Temple, after the Haihe River flooded Tianjin City in 1917.

1917年海河泛滥,水淹天津后,警察在李公祠前给灾民发馒头。

A relief kitchen set up by the local government after the flood, Tianjin, 1917.

1917年海河泛滥,洪水淹没天津后,督署设立的蒸食场。

Offering relief to the poor in the Fourth Left District, Beijing, 1920.　1920年北京内左四区粥厂放粥处

Landianchang Relief Kitchen, Beijing, 1920.

1920年北京蓝甸厂粥厂放粥处

Ciming'an Relief Kitchen, outside Fuchengmen, Beijing, 1920.

1920年北京阜城门外慈明庵粥厂

The Yellow River flooded Dongming County in July 1935. The local government sent officials to investigate damages of the flood and distribute food among refugees.

1935年7月东明县黄河水涨，县政府派人赴河西各村调查灾情并施放馍赈。

Flood victimized Jianjin County in the middle reaches of the Yangtze River in August 1935. Here, hungry people and children waiting for food.

1935年8月，长江中游水灾后，湖南省监津县被淹，灾民、儿童等待发放赈灾品。

The No. 3 Relief Kitchen in Yiyang City, Hunan, July 1935.

1935年7月长江中游水灾后，湖南省益阳城区第三施粥场。

The No. 1 Relief Kitchen in Yiyang City, Hunan, July 1935.

1935年7月长江中游水灾后，湖南省益阳城区第一施粥场。

A desilting project on the Haihe River was implemented between 1932 and 1937. Here, workers build the basement of a check gate on the Longfeng River.

1932—1937年为海河上游截流，实施海河放淤工程。图为龙凤河节制闸工程底基施工的情形。

A water gate was built on the Hutuo River in 1932 as part of the desilting project on the Haihe River.

1932年，为完成海河放淤，滹沱河水利工程水闸施工的情形。

The No.23 dam, a part of the desilting project, was completed in 1935.

1935年海河放淤工程第23号滚水坝建成后的情形

The Qujiadian Culvert, one arm of the desilting project, was completed in 1932.

1932年海河放淤工程屈家店涵洞
建成时的情形

The Yellow River diversion works in Shanxi, August 26, 1934.

1934年8月26日山西引黄工程施
工的情形

Re-enforcing the Yellow River dikes in Huoxian County, Shanxi, August 24, 1934.

1934年8月24日山西霍县加固黄
河堤岸工程。

The Third Refugee Reception Center, Ningxiang County, Hunan, July 1935.

1935年7月长江中游水灾后，湖南省宁乡县灾民第三收容所。

Strengthening the dike by binding willow tress to it, Lanfeng, Henan, July 1935.

1935年7月黄河河工在大堤挂柳护堤。图为河南省兰封小新堤工程。

The Yellow River Water Conservation Committee managed to repair the Jindi Dike in 1937. This photograph shows workers reinforcing dikes at Daokou Village, Fanxian County, Shandong.

1937年由黄河水利委员会主持培修金堤，山东范县道口村修整工程。

Strengthening the Gelou Ramp, a section of the Jindi Dike, Puxian County, Shandong, 1935.

1935年修固金堤第二段第五分段山东省濮县葛楼坡道施工情形。

A reservoir in Xinjing (present Changchun) during the Manchukuo Period.

伪满时期新京(今长春)的贮水池

Guanting Dam in 1935.

1935年官厅坝埝

Foreign water conservation experts investigating the Yellow River Project in Shanxi Province.

外国治水专家在山西视察黄河工程。

A drain bridge in Shaanxi, 1924.

1924年陕西某地的排水桥

The Dredger *Shicun* was introduced to aid the desilting project on a tributary of the Yellow River in 1935.

1935年黄河支流清淤工程引进的石村号挖泥船

Between 1934 and 1936, Li Yizhi directed construction of the Luohui Canal, Shaanxi, which irrigated an area of 500,000 mu. This photo shows a water gate on the Luohui Canal.

1934—1936年在李仪祉主持下修建的陕西洛惠渠，灌溉面积可达50万亩。图为洛惠渠排洪节制闸。

A dam on the Luohui Canal.

洛惠渠弧形拦河坝。

Between 1930 and 1932, Li Yizhi directed construction of the Jinghui Canal in the Guanzhong Area, Shaanxi. This canal irrigated 500,000 mu of farmland. Here is the Baofengsi Aqueduct.

1930年—1932年由李仪祉主持修建的陕西关中泾惠渠，灌溉面积可达50万亩。图为泾惠渠宝峰寺渡槽。

风景名胜篇

HISTORICAL SITES & SCENIC SPOTS

中华民族几千年悠久的文明史,在辽阔而古老的神州大地上,留下无数灿若星辰、令人叹为观止的遗址、遗迹:古朴稚拙的先民故居、威严庄重的宫阙、玲珑清秀的私家园林、穷奢极欲的帝王陵墓、宏伟壮观的长城古垣,以及形态各异的塔、宛若彩虹的桥、风格多样的牌坊、飞檐斗拱的亭台楼阁、远离尘世的佛门寺庙、优雅宁静的公园,等等;这些遗迹、景观的兴废,莫不留着民族盛衰的印记,无不凝聚着世代劳动人民的智慧和民族的情感。

本篇精选六十余幅照片,展示旧中国一些风景名胜。这些旧迹随着岁月的流逝,出于种种原因,或者今已发生了重大变化,或者今已不复存在,或者已经改变了原貌;相信读者读后会感慨良多……

The Chinese civilization has lasted for several thousand years. The ancient Chinese left behind a rich cultural heritage. Physical landmarks make up a significant portion of this heritage. Among these landmarks are primitive residences, magnificent palaces, elegant private gardens, superbly-constructed mausoleums of emperors, the Great Wall, various towers and pagodas, wonderful bridges, exquisite archways, gaily-painted pavilions, solemn temples, and quiet parks. These buildings record China's prosperous and hapless past.

This chapter contains approximately 60 photographs which give an overview of some of the most significant historical and scenic spots in Old China. Due to the extraordinarily long history of many of these places, some of the buildings have experienced many profound changes, some have been razed to ground and some rebuilt.

The Huanhai Zunqin Pailou (an archway), Beijing, 1901.　1901年的北京寰海尊亲牌楼

A Pailou in Chengdu.
成都的牌楼

Fuwen Pailou on Dongjiaominxiang Street, Beijing, 1901. It was removed in the 1950's.
1901年的敷文牌楼。原位于北京东交民巷,50年代被移走。

Dongsi Pailou, Beijing. This photograph was probably taken before 1934 when the original wooden arch was replaced by a concrete one in order to erect cables for trolley buses.
北京东四牌楼。该牌楼为木结构, 由两侧戗杆支撑。图系1934年改为水泥钢筋结构,以便架设电车电线以前拍摄。

Tian'anmen (Gate of Heavenly Peace). Known as Chengtian-men (Gate for Receiving Orders from Heaven) in the Ming Dynasty, it is the southern entrance to the Imperial City, home to the Ming and Qing emperors. The other three main gates include the Gate of Eastern Peace, the Gate of Western Peace, and the Gate of Earthly Peace (called Gate of Northern Peace in the Ming Dynasty). It was from Tian'anmen that emperors' edits were proclaimed before or after a grand ceremony. This photo was taken in 1901 when the allied forces of the Eight Powers invaded Beijing. Many bullet holes remain on the wall.

天安门。明代称承天门,是明清两代皇城的四座城门之一。皇城四门,南称天安门、东称东安门、西称西安门、北称地安门(明称北安门)。此门是国家举行各类大典时举行"颁诏"仪式的地方。此照摄于1901年八国联军攻入北京之后,城门上仍留着炮弹弹坑。

Tianjin Drum Tower. In ancient times, drums and bells were used to give the correct time to city residents. Therefore, every city in China had a bell and drum tower. Tianjin Drum Tower, situated in the center of the city, was destroyed by the allied forces in 1900. The drum tower shown above was rebuilt in 1921.

天津鼓楼。钟鼓楼是古代城市的报时中心。它按时撞钟,向市民报时。中国每一大中城市都设有造型各异、功能一致的钟鼓楼。图为天津三宝之一的鼓楼,位于旧城中心。该楼在1900年八国联军侵华战争中遭破坏,图系1921年修整后的天津鼓楼。

Xihuamen, the west gate to the Forbidden City. The other three gates are the Meridian Gate in the south, Donghuamen in the east, and Gate of Divine Might in the north. This photograph was taken in 1901, at which time, the Empress Dowager Cixi and Emperor Guangxu had fled to Xi'an, leaving the palace deserted.

西华门——明清两代皇宫紫禁城四座城门之一。南为午门(又名五凤楼),东为东华门,西为西华门,北为神武门(明代称玄武门)。此照摄于1901年八国联军侵入北京时,慈禧太后、光绪皇帝已逃往西安,所以宫门紧闭,荒芜凄凉。

The archway in the Temple of the Recumbent Buddha in the western suburb of Beijing.

北京西郊香山卧佛寺内的牌楼

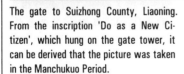

The gate to Suizhong County, Liaoning. From the inscription 'Do as a New Citizen', which hung on the gate tower, it can be derived that the picture was taken in the Manchukuo Period.

辽宁绥中县城门。从城门楼上的牌匾"作新民"可知,此照摄于伪满时期。

The south gate of Tainan City, Taiwan. 台湾台南市南大门

Donghua Gate, Shenyang City during the Russo-Japanese War, 1905.

1905年日俄战争时期的沈阳东华门

The Bell Tower of Shenyang City in the late years of the Qing Dynasty.

清光绪末年(1908年以前)的沈阳钟楼与大街。

Tianxinge is located in the southeast of Changsha City, Hunan. It' was rebuilt during the reign of Emperor Qianlong and again in 1924 when wings were erected on either side. The tower and its wings were destroyed by fire on November 12, 1938. This photograph was taken in 1924.

湖南长沙天心阁。位于长沙市东南。此阁 地势高峻,居全城之冠。建阁年代已不可考,清乾隆年间重修。1924年旧阁改建,增建两厢。1938年11月12日阁轩全部被焚毁。此照为1924年改建后所摄。

Zhengyangmen, also called Qianmen Gate Tower, is the south gate of the Inner City of Beijing and the most imposing of the city's nine gates. The photograph below shows the destroyed Qianmen Gate Tower in 1901 following the allied forces capture of Beijing.

正阳门。又称前门楼,是北京内城的正南门,它在内城九座城门中最为高大壮观。图为1901年的正阳门,八国联军攻入北京时被毁的箭楼尚未修复。

Shuzhuanglou, Datong, in the republican era.

民国时期的人同梳妆楼

Kuixinglou, Shenyang, toward the end of the Qing Dynasty.　清朝末年的沈阳魁星楼

First built in the Period of Three Kingdoms, Huanghelou (Yellow Crane Tower) is located at Huanghe Jitou, Sheshan, Wuchang. It is one of the three most famous towers in southern China. The tower was completely destroyed by a fire in 1884. This photograph was taken before the fire.

黄鹤楼。位于武昌蛇山黄鹤矶头。相传建于三国时期,历代屡修屡建,为中国江南三大名楼之一。此楼于光绪十年(1884)被焚毁。此照当为毁前所摄。

Yueyang Tower, another famous tower in the south of China, Yueyang City, Hunan. It is thought to have been built in the Period of Three Kingdoms. Later the tower was rebuilt in 1867. This photo was taken in the early republican period.

岳阳楼。位于洞庭湖畔的湘北岳阳西汀城楼上,是江南三大名楼之一。相传建于三国,为吴将鲁肃练水师的阅兵台。此楼几经兴废,清朝同治六年(1867年)重建。此照摄于民国初年。

Tengwang Tower, on the banks of the Ganjiang River, Nanchang, Jiangxi, was built in 653. The tower was immortalized by Wang Bo, a great poet of the Tang Dynasty (618 — 907). In 1926, the tower was destroyed by Deng Ruzhuo, a Northern Warlord. This picture was taken in the early republican era.

滕王阁。位于江西南昌赣江边。唐永徽四年(653年)始建,以王勃所作的《滕王阁序》而知名天下,为江南名阁之一。其后此阁屡毁屡修,直至1926年被北洋军阀邓如涿部焚毁。此照摄于民国初年。

The tomb of Han Xin (? — 196 B.C.), a famous general of the Han Dynasty (206 B.C.—23 A.D.).

韩信墓

Wanyuan Tower stands on Wuquan Mountain to the south of Lanzhou City, Gansu. The photo above was taken in 1932.

万源阁。位于甘肃兰州城南五泉山畔。此照摄于1932年。

Xiama Mausoleum lies in the south of Xi'an City. The mound in the picture belongs to Dong Zhongshu (179—104 B.C.), a master Confucian scholar of the Han Dynasty.

位于今西安市城南的下马陵，图中的冢丘，为汉代大儒董仲舒之墓。

The Temple of Confucius, located in Dongcheng District, was built in the Yuan Dynasty (1271—1368). Memorial ceremonies in honor of Confucius were held every year here during the Yuan, Ming and Qing Dynasties. Left is a photo of Dachengmen (Gate of Great Perfection) taken during the 1900's.

孔庙大成门。位于北京东城，是元、明、清三代祭祀孔子的地方，始建于元代。此照摄于清朝末年。

Huguosi Temple, in Xicheng District, Beijing, was built in the Yuan Dynasty, but later became prominent during the Qing Dynasty. This picture, taken toward the end of the Qing Dynasty, shows the Chongshoudian and Erbeiting (Pavilion of Two Stelae).

护国寺。位于北京西城，创建于元代，与东寺隆福寺相呼应，称西寺，为清朝京师名刹。此照为清末拍摄的护国寺崇寿殿与二碑亭。

The Northern Mausoleum, Mukden, lies in the north of Shenyang City, Liaoning. Also called Zhaoling Mausoleum, it belongs to Huang Taiji (1594 — 1643) and his empress. Photos 1 — 4, seen below, were taken in 1904. They show Beilou (Stele Tower), White Marble Pillar, the honorary gate, and Long'endian (Hall of Great Kindness).

奉天北陵。位于辽宁沈阳市北, 原称昭陵, 为清太宗皇太极与皇后的葬寝合陵, 是清朝关外三陵中规模最大者。照片①②③④分别为碑楼、北陵华表、牌坊、隆恩大殿。此照摄于1904年。

Wucenglou or Zhenhai Tower, located on the North Yuexiu Mountain, Guangzhou City, Guangdong, was built in 1380. The tower was repeatedly destroyed and rebuilt until it was finally rebuilt as a concrete structure in 1928. The picture was taken between 1910—1920.

五层楼。又称镇海楼, 位于广东省广州市北越秀山上, 始建于明洪武十三年(1380年), 为清朝广州八景之一。此楼历经数百年, 屡废屡修。1928年重修时改内部的砖木结构为钢筋水泥结构。此照摄于清末民初。

Lingze Temple dedicated to the wife of Sun Quan (182 — 252), he being the founder of the Wu Kingdom in the Period of Three Kingdoms.

孙权夫人灵泽庙

The Temple of Confucius, Xi'an. Built in 1090, the temple is located near Xiama Mausoleum in the southern part of the city. It is now called the Museum of Stelae, for its rich and valuable collection of stelae, dating back to the Tang Dynasty. The photo below was taken in 1934 before the Xitong Railway was laid.

西安孔庙。位于西安市城南下马陵,建于宋朝元祐五年(1090年),内收唐开成石经。经历代收集,蔚然成一碑林。现改称为"碑林博物馆"。此照摄于1934年修建西潼铁路之前。

Standing on the South Street, Xingcheng, Liaoning, the two arches, in honor of the Zu family, were erected in 1638. Zu Dashou and Zu Dale were brave generals who defended China against Manchu invasions. There is, however, some irony in the fact that the two generals surrendered to Manchu rulers after the Songshan Defeat in 1642.

民国初年的祖氏牌坊。位于辽宁兴城内南大街,共两座,一南一北,为明朝抗金将领祖大寿、祖大乐兄弟的功德牌坊,建于明朝崇祯十一年(1638年),造型深厚,生动宏伟。此牌坊原是明崇祯皇帝为鼓励祖氏兄弟保卫辽东所建,然而祖氏兄弟于崇祯十五年(1642年)松山之战时降清,此事遂成历史笑柄。

Wuhouci (Temple of the Count of Wu) is dedicated to Zhuge Liang (184 — 234), Prime Minister of the Shu Kingdom in the Period of Three Kingdoms. The temple is located in the east of Bocheng, Mianxian County, Shaanxi where the Prime Minister died from constant overwork. This photo was taken in 1934.

武侯祠。位于陕西勉县伯城东。三国时蜀丞相诸葛亮葬于勉县定军山下,故于此立祠以祭。此照摄于1934年修建西潼铁路之前。

The Mausoleum of King Wen, who paved the way for the founding of the Zhou Dynasty (1111? — 246 B.C.), is located in the northwest of Xi'an City. Archeological research has, however, revealed a possible misnomer. It is heavily speculated that this tomb was built long after the death of King Wen, and therefore does not in fact house his body.

周文王陵。位于今西安西北,相传为周文王陵,图上陵碑为清朝陕西巡抚毕沅所树。然此陵定名有误。据考古勘察证实,此陵系秦国(战国)时期的墓葬。

Under the supervision of the Qing government, the Temple of Li Hongzhang was built in 1905 in honor of the former governor of Zhili (present Hebei).

天津李(鸿章)公祠。1905年为祭清朝直隶总督李鸿章修建的专祠。

A reliquary in Huangling County, Shaanxi, which is said to house several articles of clothing of the Yellow Emperor, regarded by most Chinese as the first great ruler of China.

古轩辕黄帝陵。位于陕西黄陵县,相传是中华民族的先祖轩辕黄帝归天后的衣冠冢。

The Sacred Way to the Ming Tombs, Changping County, Beijing.

明陵神路。位于北京昌平县,是通往明朝十三陵的神道。

Chengongci, Guangnan, Yunnan.
云南广南府陈公祠

Chang'an Temple of Shenyang City during the Russo-Japanese War, 1905.
1905年日俄战争时期的沈阳城内长安寺

Jiantan Temple, Taibei City, Taiwan.
台湾台北市剑潭寺

The Fengmen Twin Stupa standing in Dinghui Temple, Suzhou City, Jiangsu, was built by Wang Wenhan and his brother in 984 — 987. One is called Stupa and the other is Beneficence Stupa. The photo below was taken in the early years of the Republic of China.

江苏封门双塔。位于江苏苏州市城南定慧寺，宋朝雍熙年间(984—987)吴县王文罕兄弟所建，一名舍利塔，一名功德舍利塔。此照摄于民国初年。

Liurong Pagoda stands in Liurong Temple, the center part of Guangzhou City, Guangdong. Octagonal and eight-storied, the pagoda was built in 537, and rebuilt during the Northern Song Dynasty (969 — 1127). From the top, visitors have a full view of the city. This photo was taken in the early republican period.

六榕塔。位于广东广州市六榕寺内，又称花塔。初建于梁朝大同三年(537年)，北宋时重建，为八角九级砖木结构。此塔位于市中心，登顶可俯览广州城景。此照摄于民国初年。

The Five-Pagoda is located in the Five-Pagoda Temple, Huhhot City, Inner Mongolia. The pagoda, 15 meters high, was built during the reign of the Yongzheng Emperor (Qing Dynasty 1723 — 1735). On each corner of the Diamond Throne, there is a five-storied pagoda, and a center pagoda which is seven stories high. This picture was taken in 1932.

五塔。位于今内蒙古呼和浩特旧城五塔寺内。建于清朝雍正年间(1723—1735年)，塔高15米，砖石结构。金刚座上设五座塔，居中者为七层塔，四角各为五层小塔。此系1932年拍摄的五塔中的一小塔。

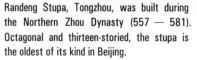

Randeng Stupa, Tongzhou, was built during the Northern Zhou Dynasty (557 — 581). Octagonal and thirteen-storied, the stupa is the oldest of its kind in Beijing.

通州燃灯舍利塔。建于北周(557—581年)，八角十三层，为北京最古老的佛塔之一。

Huangsi Pagoda is located in the West Huang (Yellow Sect of Buddhism) Temple, Andingmenwai, Beijing. The temple, built in 1723, was the residence of Dalai and Panchen Lamas as well as other important Tibetan officials during their visits to Beijing. In 1780, the Sixth Panchen Lama came to Beijing and attended the birthday celebration of Emperor Qianlong, but died of smallpox while still in the capital city. Two years later, the Qing government built a memorial pagoda for him, named "Qingjing Huacheng".

黄寺塔。位于北京安定门外西黄寺内。西黄寺始建于清朝雍正元年(1723年)，为藏传佛教达赖、班禅及其他官员来京的住所。乾隆六年(1780年)班禅六世来京为乾隆祝大寿，因出天花在此圆寂。后清朝政府于1782年在此为班禅六世建衣冠塔，命名为"清净化诚塔"。

The Great Wild Goose Pagoda stands in Daci'ensi Temple, in a southern suburb of Xi'an City. The 64-meter-high pagoda was built in the Tang Dynasty. The picture above was taken in 1904.

大雁塔。位于西安南郊的大慈恩寺内，塔高64米，是唐代遗留下来的著名佛塔。此照摄于1904年。

Gaoliang Bridge. Constructed with stone blocks, the single-span bridge, situated in Xizhimenwai, lying across the Gaoliang River, Beijing, was rebuilt in the Qing Dynasty. This photo was taken in the late Qing Dynasty.

高粱桥。位于北京西直门外,因桥跨古高粱河而得名。始建年代不可考,清代重建,为青白石单孔拱桥。此照摄于清朝末年。

The Ancient Passage Bridge or Puji Bridge spans on the Fengshui River, which flows between Xi'an and Xianyang, Shaanxi Province. It was built in the Reign of Qianlong Emperor Qing Dynasty. This photo was taken in 1934 before the construction of Xitong Railway.

咸阳古渡桥。位于陕西西安与咸阳之间沣水之上,又称普济桥,清乾隆时建。此照摄于1934年西潼铁路修建之前。

Huayuan Bridge, built on the busy Suzhou River, led to the foreign concession areas of Shanghai.

上海苏州河花园桥。此桥横跨上海繁华地区的苏州河,连接被苏州河隔开的英国等国共同租界区。

This wooden bridge is the only entrance to the deep and secluded valleys of the picturesque Jizu Mountain, a well-known scenic spot in Yunnan Province.

位于云南省鸡足山风景区的钓桥。此桥可引游人到对面风景优美的幽谷中去,别无他路。桥面两旁全是木制桥栏。

The Fifteen-Arch Bridge, Jinan, during the republican era.

民国时期的济南十五孔桥

Shamian Bridge, Guangzhou.

民国时期的广州市沙面桥

Dajing Pass and Zhangjiakou Great Wall. Built in 1485, Dajing Pass, located in a deep valley in Zhangjiakou City, was of great military importance during the Ming Dynasty.

大境门及张家口长城。位于河北张家口市,原为明代长城的一个关隘,修建于明朝成化二十一年(1485年),此门处于两山交接的山谷之中,为历代兵家必夺之军事要隘。此照摄于清朝末年。

The City Wall of Nanjing. The largest of its kind in the world, the city wall was constructed between 1366 and 1386. It is 33.65 kilometers long, 14 to 21 meters high, 14 meters thick at the base, and 7 meters broad on top. The picture above was taken in the early republican period.

南京城垣。建于元朝至正二十六年(1366年)至明朝洪武十九年(1386年),全长33.65公里,高14—21米不等,基宽14米,顶宽7米,蔚为壮观,为世界第一城墙。图为其中一段,摄于民国初年。

The French Garden, Tianjin.
天津法国花园

Shanghai Park, 1919.
1919的上海公园

Shanghai Zhangyuan Garden, 1919.
1919年的上海张园

Yuanmingyuan, one of the summer palaces of the Qing emperors, was actually three separate parks: Yuanmingyuan (Park of Perfection and Brightness), Wanchunyuan (Park of Ten Thousand Springs), and Changchunyuan (Park of Everlasting Spring). Its construction started in 1709 and took 150 years to complete. Against a backdrop of great natural beauty, buildings in Chinese and Western styles embodied the most refined techniques of Chinese art and architecture. It was the absolute splendor of the Yuanmingyuan which earned it the nickname "the park of parks". Unfortunately, in 1860, the Anglo-French joint forces looted all the treasures in the park and set fire to it. In 1900, the allied forces of the Eight Powers sacked the remaining buildings, reducing this famous creation to smoldering ruins. The photo above was taken between 1860 and 1900.

圆明园是清朝皇帝夏宫之一，包括圆明园、长春园、万春园，始建于康熙三十九年(1700年)，陆续修建达150余年。此园集古今中外园林建筑风格特色，号称"万园之园"，园内收藏举世无双。1860年、1900年两度遭西方列强焚烧洗劫，已成一片废墟。此照摄于1860年——1900年之间。

Qinhuai Canal. Located in Nanjing, Jiangsu, the canal, about 110 kilometers long, was built in the Period of Three Kingdoms. The busiest area along the canal was at the Confucius Temple in Nanjing City, where restaurants, brothels, stalls and shops were heavily clustered.

秦淮河。位于江苏南京,相传秦始皇开凿,故名秦淮。实为三国时孙吴所开。全长110公里。秦淮河在南京城内以夫子庙一带最繁盛,遍布酒家妓院、摊店货栈,成为吃喝玩乐的代名词。

Songhua River in Harbin City, Heilongjiang. The bridge in the distance was built by Russia in 1901.

夏天的黑龙江哈尔滨市松花江岸。远处江上的大桥,是1901年沙俄修建的哈尔滨第一松花江古桥。此照摄于1932年。

The mineral spring in Huaqing Palace, Lintong, Shaanxi, is remnant of the Tang Dynasty. This photo was taken in 1904.

陕西临潼的骊山华清宫贵妃池是唐朝遗迹。此照摄于1904年。

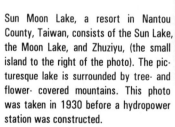

Sun Moon Lake, a resort in Nantou County, Taiwan, consists of the Sun Lake, the Moon Lake, and Zhuziyu, (the small island to the right of the photo). The picturesque lake is surrounded by tree- and flower- covered mountains. This photo was taken in 1930 before a hydropower station was constructed.

日月潭。位于台湾南投县群山之中,是著名的风景区。潭中有珠仔屿(即照片右侧小岛),北为日潭,南为月潭,以轮廓形似日月而得名。潭水周围,林木扶疏,翠峰环抱,山水交映。此照摄于1930年,水电工程修建之前。

街景篇

STREETS

　　在华夏这片大地上,大大小小的城镇星罗棋布,它们或是历史文化名城,或是某一地区的军政中心,或是新兴的商埠,或是交通的枢纽,或者是上述这些的总和。城市又是由四通八达的街道交织起来的,城市的特色也是通过不同风貌的街道表现出来的,因此,街景成为透视城市政治、经济、文化生活的一个重要窗口。可以这么说:街道是城市的血脉,而街道旁的政府机构是城市的精神中枢,街道旁的店铺是城市的活力所在。

　　本篇这组照片着重反映街景,力图使读者透过这些街景,管窥旧中国若干城市的风貌。这些街景随着时间的推移和时代的变迁,绝大多数早已不复存在,或早已面目全非,今天目睹这些留在照片上的历史陈迹,时空仿佛倒流,我们又重新站在了那些十字街头,置身于饭馆、旅店、布庄、当铺之中,摊棚林立,百货杂陈;眼前仿佛展现出当年的灯红酒绿、车水马龙、招幌翻舞的景象,耳中充盈着红男绿女的熙熙攘攘、商贾伙计的吆喝叫卖之声……或者是截然相反的另一番景象:贫困落后、偏僻边远的小城,泥泞的街道,破烂的店面,凌乱的杂货摊,冷冷清清,一片萧条……

　　为了尽可能全面地反映大、中、小各类城市的街景,本篇选择的城市包括东北、华北、西北、西南、华东、华中、华南等各大区,上至京师、上海、天津、武汉、西安、广州等大城市,下至边陲小镇,涵盖面极广;街道的种类包括商业街景、行政区街景、租界区街景等,种类齐全。

There are thousands of towns and cities in China. Some of them are famous for historical events, some are populous and prosperous, some are political and military centers, and some traffic hubs. Within a city, roads and streets not only provide a place to walk or drive, but also mirror features of the area. If streets can be regarded as arteries of a city, then the government building standing on the main road can be considered the nerve center, and the shops and stalls which line the streets become its nerves.

This chapter attempts to restore the old appearance of some streets which have taken on a new look or are no longer in existence. The pages are designed to allow the reader to take a leisurely stroll down an old Chinese street. In order to provide an accurate overview of Old China, this chapter contains photos from a wide variety of cities—big or small, dynamic or stagnant scattered all over China. Streets in administrative areas and foreign concessions are also included.

Sulang Street, Dalian, Liaoning
Province, in the republican period.

民国时期辽宁大连浪速街

Gulou Street, Beijing, in the republican period.

民国时期北京鼓楼大街

A street in Changping County, Beijing, while under Japanese rule.

日伪时期昌平街景

A street in Wanping, while under Japanese rule. This photograph was taken after 1940 when the puppet North China Government Administrative Commission was founded.

日伪时期宛平街景。街上的日本太阳旗和伪"华北政务委员会"的五色旗说明,照片摄于1940年之后。

A business street in Miyun County, Beijing, in the republican period.　民国时期密云街市

Dongjiaominxiang Street, the legation quarter in Beijing, in the republican period. Left is a Japanese bank and right is a hotel.

民国时期北京外国使馆区东交民巷街，左边为日本正金银行，右边为六国饭店。

A business street in Tongxian County, Beijing, in the republican period.

民国时期通县街市

Huairou County, Beijing, in the republican period.

民国时期怀柔街景

Nanjing Street was Shanghai's most bustling business area in the republican period. When this photo was taken, shopkeepers on the street were on strike.

民国时期上海最繁华的南京路。由于拍摄此照时商店罢市，街面上显得冷冷清清，全无往日熙熙攘攘，车水马龙的热闹景象。

The Japanese Concession in Tianjin was set up in 1896. It was located on the south bank of the Haihe River, next to the French Concession. Today's Heping Street was called the Sun Street during the concession period.

天津日本租界1896年建立，位于海河南岸，与法国租界相隔。图为民国时期天津日本租界旭街（今和平路）。

Harbin, Heilongjiang, in Manchukuo period.

伪满时期黑龙江哈尔滨街景

Hongkou Department Store,
Shanghai, in the republican era.

民国时期上海虹口市场

The French Concession in Tianjin was set
up in 1861. It was located on the south
bank of the Haihe River, between the
Japanese and British concessions. Here is
a street in the concession during the republican era.

天津法国租界1861年建立，位于
海河南岸、英日租界之间。图为民
国时期天津法国租界大马路

The French Concession in Shanghai
in the republican period.

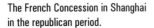

民国时期上海法国租界区街景

Around the Drum Tower, Suiyuan, in the republican period.

民国时期绥远鼓楼附近的街景

Zhangjiakou was an important town in Chahar Province, in the republican period.

民国时期边关重镇察哈尔张家口街景

Chengde, Jehol Province, while under Japanese rule.

日伪时期热河承德街景

Tai'an, Shandong, in the republican era.

民国时期山东泰安街景

Sipailou, Datong, Shanxi, in the republican period.

民国时期山西大同四牌楼一带街景

Around the Drum Tower, Xi'an in the republican period.

民国时期陕西西安鼓楼附近街景

The Central Street, Xilin, Jehol Province, in the republican period.

民国时期热河林西
(今属内蒙古) 中央大街

Hailar City, Heilongjiang (Presently in the Inner Mongolia Autonomous Region), in the republican period.

民国时期的黑龙江(今属内蒙古)
海拉尔市街景。

Chifeng, Inner Mongolia, in the republican period.

民国时期内蒙古赤峰街景

Yanji, Jilin, during the Manchuko period.
伪满时期吉林延吉街景

民国时期辽宁朝阳街景
Chaoyang, Liaoning Province,
in the republican period.

Manzhouli, Heilongjiang (Presently in the
Inner Mongolia Autonomous Region) in
the republican period.

民国时期黑龙江满洲里
(今属内蒙古)街景

The concession area of Tianjin in the Period of the Republic of China. After the Second Opium War in 1860, Britain established the first concession in Tianjin. Later other imperialist nations including France, America, Germany, Japan, Russia, Belgium, Italy and Austria also founded their concessions in the city where they built many buildings in their native designs.

民国时期天津租界区街市。1860年第二次鸦片战争后，英国首先在天津开外国租界，继而法、美、德、日、俄、比、意、奥在津建立租界。各国在其租界内，按照各自不同的建筑艺术风格修建，形成了天津各国租界内独特的街景。

Shanghaiguan Pass in the republican period.　　民国时期山海关城内街景

Baotou, Inner Mogolia, in the republican period.　　民国时期内蒙古包头街景

Chongwenman area, Beijing, in 1940 when the Japanese-controlled North China Government Administrative Commission was founded.

日伪时期伪"华北政务委员会"成立时(1940年)的北京崇文门一带街景。

Tsitsihar, Heilongjiang in the Manchukuo Period.　伪满时期黑龙江齐齐哈尔街景

Jinan, Shandong, in the republican period.　民国时期山东济南街景

Penglai, Shandong, in the republican period.

民国时期山东莱州街景

Yantai, Shandong, in the republican period.

民国时期山东烟台街景

Xinjiekou, the central area of Nanjing, Jiangsu, in 1946.

1946年江苏南京中心区新街口

Menzi, Yunnan, in the republican period.

民国时期云南蒙自街景

Qinhuai Canal, a bustling business area, in Nanjing, Jiangsu, in the republican period.

民国时期江苏南京闹市区秦淮河街景

Ningbo, Zhejiang, in the republican period.

民国时期浙江宁波街景

A Chinese street, Hong Kong.

香港华人街

Xinzhu, Taiwan, while under the
colonial rule of Japan.

日本殖民时期台湾新竹街景

Yonghan Street, the busiest area in Guangzhou,
Guangdong, in the republican period.

民国时期广东广州最繁华的永汉马路

Daping Street, Taipei, Taiwan, while under the colonial rule of Japan.

日本殖民时期台湾台北大平街街 景

Yizhong Street, Keelong, Taiwan, while under the colonial rule of Japan.

日本殖民时期台湾基隆义重大街

Taichung, Taiwan, while under the colonial rule of Japan.

日本殖民时期台湾台中街景

Changsha, Hunan in the republican period.　民国时期湖南长沙街景

民国时期江西九江西门一带街景
A street near the West Gate of Jiujiang
City, Jiangxi, in the republican period.

Nanchang, Jiangxi, in the republican period.

民国时期江西南昌街景

The downtown area of Hankou, a section of Wuhan, Hubei,
in the republican period.

民国时期湖北武汉三镇之一的汉口闹市区街景

Tainan, Taiwan, while under Japanese colonization.

日本殖民时期台湾台南街景

Guangzhou, Guangdong, in the republican period.

民国时期广东广州街景

Shaoxing, Zhejiang, in the republican period.

民国时期浙江绍兴城内的水上街景

Kunming, Yunnan, in the republican period.
民国时期云南昆明街景

Wuchang, the cultural area of Wuhan, Hubei, in the republican period.
民国时期湖北武汉三镇之一的文化区武昌街景

Dali, Yunnan, in the republican period.
民国时期云南大理街景

服饰篇

CLOTHES AND ACCESSORIES

"衣、食、住、行"是人类生存繁衍的最根本的内容,服装不仅是生活的必需品,也是人类走向文明的标志。

中外古今,人们的服饰风格各异,千姿百态;本篇精选六十余幅照片,集中反映旧中国各民族、各阶层的服饰,主要分以下几大类:

晚清服饰:自清初剃发易服,清朝的衣冠之俗垂承几百年,基本没有大的变化。这部分主要反映清末满族妇女服饰,如旗袍、高底鞋(俗称"花盆底"或"马蹄底")、仿慈禧高大髻式在满族贵妇中盛行一时的"达拉翅"头式等等;清末汉族妇女的服饰,头式多为盘头,上身袄衫下身束裙或长裤,一般掩及脚部,缠足三寸金莲,颇具明代汉族服装遗风;此外还选录了少量女官服、蒙古族服饰、满汉男子便服、儿童服装等;

民国服饰:随着封建帝制被推翻,满族统治的失败,人们的服饰起了很大的变化,男子或西服加长袍"中西合璧",或西服革履一派"洋务",或长袍马褂的"国粹派",或全副中山装的革命党人形象;女子先是时兴高领袄衫,继而时兴新式高开叉无袖旗袍,五颜六色,绚烂夺目;一时中西满汉,异彩纷呈,服饰新潮一浪高过一浪;

艺术服饰:此类服饰多用于舞台,属艺术化装束,非家居生活实用。

Clothing, along with food, and housing, is one of the basic necessities for survival. Moreover, clothes provide deep insight into a civilization.

This chapter contains more than 60 photographs showing different styles of dress for varied nationalities and classes. Also contained in this chapter are costumes for stage performance. The chapter is divided into two sections.

The late Qing Period. With the establishment of the Qing Dynasty, Manchu rulers forced the Han to adopt their style of dress. Few changes occurred during the following two and half centuries. Typical style of dress for a Manchu woman in the late Qing period was composed of a Qipao, a vest, a pair of horse-hoof shoes and also the quaint headdress called Dalachi. Clothes for Han women in the Qing dynasty maintained many of the features found during the Ming Dynasty. A Han woman in this period normally wore a jacket, and a long skirt or a pair of trousers — long enough to cover her so-called "three-inch" feet, which were bound in her youth. The republican era. Accompanying the fall of the Manchu Empire was a great change in the style of dress. In addition to the traditional Manchu garments, men also wore Western-style suits and tunic suits. Women in the early years of this period preferred first high collared jackets, then sleeveless Qipaos with high slits up the sides, and later a great diverse array of fashionable clothes.

A young Manchu woman in the standard fashion during the Qing Dynasty. The women usually wore a long garment, called a Qipao, and a sleeveless jacket trimmed with bright-colored lace and buttons.

清代满族少女头发梳理成两把头式．装饰非常讲究，身着马甲旗袍的镶边、锁扣色彩对比精美。

This type of headdress, called Dalachi, was very popular among noble Manchu women in the Qing Dynasty.

清代满族贵妇头饰均为流行的达拉翅,背坐者展示了达拉翅后边的梳理方式。

Clothes of noble Manchu women in the Qing Dynasty were exquisitely made, especially the lace on Qipao and jacket.

清代满族贵妇服饰做工异常考究,尤其是马甲、旗袍的边饰更为精美。

Headdress and clothes of noble Manchu women vary greatly.

清代满族贵妇每人头戴的达拉翅,各个均有明显变化,服饰马甲亦有特色。

Clothes of Manchu noble women and children toward the end of the Qing.

清末满族贵妇及其子弟的服饰

Winter clothes of Manchu women. The painted mouth, small and red like a cherry, was in vogue in the Qing Dynasty.

清代满族妇女冬装旗袍、马甲,款式均不同。当时崇尚"樱桃小口一点点",故每人口涂盈红。

Clothes worn by the esteemed Manchu women and children in the late Qing. In addition to the richly decorated headdress, there were exquisite Qipao, vest, and horse-hoof shoes made of high quality silk. High collars were also the fashion.

清末满族妇女儿童服饰,所展示的除贵妇头饰上华美的达拉翅外,身着的马甲旗袍质地也很精良,高脖领是当时的时尚,脚穿花盆底鞋。

Dress of a Manchu woman and her child in the Qing Dynasty.

清代满族妇女及其子弟的服饰

The summer dress of Manchu women in the Qing Dynasty and their horse-hoof shoes.

清代满族贵妇夏季服饰简洁、明快,脚穿高底鞋。

Women's headdress toward the end of the Qing Dynasty with no fringe and the winter garment has a high collar.

清末妇女的头饰前额无留海,为两把头式,身着高脖领冬季旗袍。

A noble Manchu woman holding her baby.

怀抱婴儿的清末满族贵妇着装

The headdress of noble Manchu women is often decorated with a large peony flower on Dalachi, and many small peach flowers on the right side of the forehead.

清末满族贵妇头戴的达拉翅，中间镶嵌大朵牡丹花，右前额缀满无数桃红花朵。

Dress of Han women in the Qing Dynasty consisted of a long gown, a long skirt, and a pair of trousers. Hem on the gowns varied greatly.

清代汉族妇女服饰，外长褂、长裙，内长裤，主要变化仍然是在服装的边饰上。

Hair tied in a knot was a popular coiffure among married Han women in the Qing Dynasty.

清代汉族妇女头发盘髻的照片

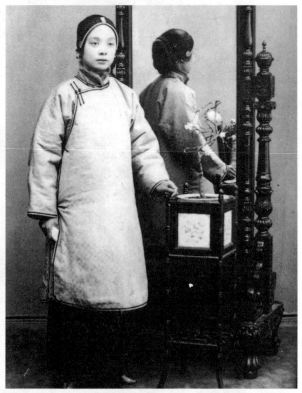

Summer dress for Han women in the Qing Dynasty.　　清代汉族青年女子夏季服饰

Clothes of a Han woman and child.　　清代汉族妇女儿童服饰

Old Han women wore velvet hats and fur coats in winter.

清代汉族老年妇女头戴平绒毡帽,身着皮毛冬袄。

A Han family in the Qing Dynasty. Right are the grandmother with her grandson and to their left her daughter-in-low.

这是一个清代汉族家庭的合影。右坐为长,膝下为孙,左为儿媳。从他们的服饰上可看出满汉服饰文化的交融。

Different coiffures of young and old Han women.

清代汉族少妇头饰留海,后盘髻,老年妇女前额光光,后也盘髻。

Winter dress of the Hans
during the 1910's.

清末民初汉族冬季服饰

New-fashioned high
collar gowns for
women in the early
republican era.

民初新式高领女装

Formal dress of wives of
high-ranking off cials
worn during an audience
with the monarch.

清末诰命夫人朝服

Everyday dress of the
wives of court officials.

清末诰命夫人便装

Summary dress and hair style in the early republican era is quite different from those of the Qing Dynasty.

民国初年的夏季女装较清代有了很大改变,头发的梳理也颇不同。

Summer dress during the 1930's. 民国时期妇女高领袖夏季服饰

The women's Western-style fur coat during the 1930's

民国时期妇女西式裘皮冬装服饰

Women wore sleeveless Qipao during the 1930's.

民国时期妇女的高开叉无袖夏季旗袍

Gown for Manchu men in the reign of
Emperor Guangxu Qing Dynasty, 1896.

1896年(光绪丙申年)间男子冬季
旗装

Winter gown for Man-
chu men in the 1900's.

清末男子冬季旗装

Men's dress in the
early republican era.
民初男子服饰

Winter dress for upper class
men during the late Qing Dynasty.
清末上层男子冬季服装

Summer dress for men during the 1900's.
清末男子夏季服饰

Winter dress for men
in the late Qing Dynasty.

清末男子冬装

Dress for lower class men
in the late Qing Dynasty.

清末下层男子服饰

Winter dress for Manchus
in late Qing Dynasty.

清末满族男女冬季服饰

The new army uniform of the Qing; Manchu gown and formal dress for the wife
of a high-ranking official.

清末军装、旗服、女官服饰。左女
为诰命夫人，着官服。中间长者着
男子旗装；右边青年男子着清朝
新式军服。

Clothes of Han people
in late Qing Dynasty.

清末汉族男女服饰

A Han family at the end of the Qing.
清末汉族家庭服饰

Winter dress for Han people
in the late Qing Dynasty.
清末汉族男女冬装

Everyday dress at the end of the Qing.
清末家庭服饰

Typically-dressed people in the later Qing
Dynasty

清末男女服饰。妇女均上着长袄，
下着裙子。

A Han family at the end of the Qing.

清末汉族家庭众生相

Children's dress
at the end of the
Qing Dynasty.

清末儿童服饰

Manchu dress toward the end of the Qing.

清末满族男女服饰

The coiffure of Manchu women in the republican era, was quite different from Dalachi, the headdress popular among noble Manchu women in the late Qing Dynasty.

民国时期满族妇女头饰, 它与清末满族贵妇的达拉翅不同, 而是民间化地向上做成空心状。

A peasant woman in Siping, Northeast China, in the republican period.

民国初期东北四平农家妇女服饰

Mongolian women in their festival clothing in the republican period.

民国时期蒙族盛装妇女，头饰异常奇特。

Clothes of common Mongolian women in the republican period.

民国时期蒙族普通妇女服饰

Mongolian women of the upper class in the republican period.

民国时期蒙族上层妇女服饰

In the south and southwest of China, men often wore turbans in the republican period.

民国时期四川男子头饰。中国西南、华南地区的成年男子习惯以青布缠头,缠法各有不同。

In the republican era, women in Zhangzhou, Fujian, wore three knives in the hair for decoration as well as self-defense. Here is the so called Three-Knife Headdress.

民国时期福建漳州妇女头饰,称为三把刀,因其上方及左右各有小尖刀形头饰,以抵御强暴。

Dress of performing artists. 艺人、妓女着艺装.

Costumes for women.

妇女戏装

The rich headdress and clothing of a Han woman.

清末汉族妇女节日盛装时的头饰
和服饰

Costumes for the vivacious
female role in Peking Opera.

清末京剧花旦戏装

Costumes for the
old male role in
Peking Opera.

京剧老生戏装

Costumes of the famous Shibuxian Troupe in the late Qing Dynasty.

清朝末年什不闲戏班的戏装

Dress of vaudevillians in the early republican era.

民国初年杂耍艺人服饰

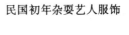

Costumes for the female roles in Sichuan Opera toward the end of the Qing.

清朝末年的川戏旦角服装

民俗篇 CUSTOMS

中华民族有几千年的悠久历史,各地区、各民族都有着丰富灿烂的民俗文化,这些民俗千差万别,有着丰富的内涵。本篇收集了大量反映旧中国民俗习惯的照片,从中可以管窥旧中国民众的日常生活。

这组照片包括衣食住行各个方面的风俗习惯风行时尚,诸如豪华奢侈的祝寿场面、喜庆欢乐的婚娶仪式、隆重排场的丧葬出殡,等等;与日常生活息息相关的种类繁多的出行代步工具,如轿子、马车、牛车、人力车、新式汽车等;各民族因地制宜的居住场所,如窑洞、蒙古包、穴居等。

另外,还收集了一些反映传统节日中耍狮子、划旱船等娱乐活动的情景以及上至达官贵人,下至贫民百姓调剂生活的业余爱好和消遣的照片,等等。

在旧中国的风俗中,还夹杂着一些低级甚至丑恶的内容,诸如卖淫、嫖娼、赌博、抽大烟、占卜算卦、祈神驱鬼,等等;为了真实、全面地反映旧中国的风俗,这些也适当地收录了一些。

China's history, one of the longest on earth, spans a period of several thousand years. Customs, which are derived from both social and cultural development, differ greatly among various nationalities and locations in China. This chapter illustrates the daily life of the Chinese people in history.

This chapter also provides an overview of traditional ceremonies, classical and modern means of transportation, different types of dwellings found throughout China, as well as Chinese folk dances. In an attempt to give a complete overview of the customs in Old China, this chapter also depicts the darker elements such as prostitution, gambling, and opium addiction.

Making offerings to the
God of Wealth on the Eve
of the Spring Festival is a
tradition in the Northeast
of China.

东北地区大年三十晚
祭财神的贡桌

Such superstitions as physiognomy, sortilege and divination have a very long history in China. Here is a fortune teller.

抽签相面、求神问鬼等占卜算卦是中国古老的迷信活动。图为人道旁为行人算卦者。

A birthday party for the senior member of an upper class family. Here, the spacious dining hall is decorated with longevity couplets and works of calligraphy and painting.

为老年人祝寿，是中国传统的民俗礼仪活动。图为清末上层人物祝寿时的寿堂。从图面上看，四面祝寿锦帐，中有祝寿对联和字画，下摆多张筵桌，异常奢侈排场。

The first day of the lunar year, known as the Spring Festival, is the most important traditional festival in China. In Northeast China, people beat gongs and drums for the God of Wealth to ensure a prosperous year.

农历正月初一过年，又称春节，是中国传统节令之中最重要的节日，迎新辞旧是主要节日内容。图为中国东北地区民俗，大年三十敲锣鼓迎财神，以求来年财源广进。

In preparation for the Spring Festival, people buy food and other special goods. Here is a shopper from the outskirts of Beijing.

临近年关时，中国民俗传统是采办年货，将节日的衣食安排得丰富、新鲜，以求欢乐迎新。图为北京城外采购年货者。

People in Northeast China welcome in the God of Wealth on the new-year's eve and pray for a prosperous year.

图为中国东北民俗，大年三十晚焚香叩头，迎接财神，以求来年财源茂盛的接神仪式。

A western-style wedding, Beijing, while under the rule of Japan. The new couple are both members of the upper class. There were large crowds to cheer the new pair.

日伪时期北京某官僚子女西式婚礼情景。新郎西装革履，新娘白纱红花。这与中国传统的新郎长袍马褂十字披红、新娘凤冠霞帔身着旗袍、红衣红袄呈明显对照。

According to funeral rites of the Han people, relatives of the deceased should wear mourning apparel to express their grief. Here are women and children in their mourning apparel.

汉族传统的丧葬仪式中，为寄托对于死者的哀思，死者的后代、亲属要身着丧服，披麻戴孝。图为穿着丧服的妇女和儿童。

In old times, people placed a great value on funerals. A grand funeral was normally regarded as the expression of heartfelt respect for the deceased. In old Beijing, there used to be a special business called Gangfang — offering funeral services. Here is a funeral of the highest order. The coffin is carried by 128 people.

扛房是北京旧时专门承办丧礼出殡的行业，为了显示死者的身份和地位，以及后人对死者丧事的态度，出殡时有十六扛(指抬棺材的人数，二人为一扛)、三十二扛、六十四扛之分。图为最高档次的六十四扛出殡场面。

The streamer-like objects shown in the photograph below are often used in wedding and funeral ceremonies as well as official processions. They are symbols of auspiciousness and extravagance.

打幡是中国民间传统的红白喜事中礼仪队伍的一部分，也用于官方仪仗，是一种象征吉利而招摇过市的仪仗。

Moslem funeral rites are quite different from those of the Hans. Here is a Moslem funeral in the republican period.

穆斯林的传统丧葬习惯与汉族不同。图为民国时期北京清真公益出殡的场面。

Sheep skin rafts are a major form of transportation in the upper reaches of the Yellow River.

黄河上的皮筏子。河工用完整的羊皮充气,捆扎成人羊皮筏子,这是黄河上游民间普遍多见的渡河交通工具。

In the upper reaches of the Yalu River, people tie such rafts to transport logs.

鸭绿江上游的筏子。这种木筏,往往是为顺水运输木材而扎成的,做交通工具不是主要目的。

In winter, sleds are commonly used for transportation in Northeast China. Here is a sleigh on the frozen Songhua River.

中国东北的冬季,冰封千里,舟车难行,当地习惯以爬犁为代步运输工具。图为松花江上的爬犁车。

A cart being pulled by a camel.

长城外用骆驼拉的轿车

A wheelbarrow commonly seen in Shandong.

山东独轮车

Such hand carts with sails can employ wind to save men power.

带帆的手推车，这种手推车可以借助风力，省力轻捷。

A cradle. 摇篮

A woman
riding a donkey.
妇人骑驴。

Tourists hired such sedan chairs, carried by four men, to go sight-seeing at the West Lake, Hangzhou.

西湖爬山轿，是四人抬的山舆，专供游人登山乘坐。

The ox-drawn cart was widely used in rural areas toward the end of the Qing Dynasty.

清末农村双套牛车，车轮多为木制，外边有铁箍，行进时笨重、震动大。

Ox-drawn carts.

柳条制的围子车

In the Loess Plateau area such as Shaanxi and Shanxi, many people live in Yaodong, a kind of cave house.

陕西、山西等黄土高原地带，民居多是窑洞。图为陕西乡间破旧的窑洞。

A rural mud house.

农村土坯房

This fixed yurt is built with wood and earth.

固定蒙古包。这种蒙古包为土木结构，无法迁移。

A farmer in the late Qing Dynasty.

清末农民手持耙搂, 肩负背篓, 外出劳作时的情形。

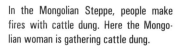
In the Mongolian Steppe, people make fires with cattle dung. Here the Mongolian woman is gathering cattle dung.

蒙古草原上, 树木稀少, 民间取火, 多以牛粪为燃料。图为蒙族妇女肩负背篓外出拾牛粪的情形。

Grounding grain with a stone roller.
推碾子加工粮食的情形

In the eastern region of Inner Mongolia, people built wooden water channels to prevent water from soaking into the sand.

在内蒙东部为防止水渗入沙中，将圆木凿槽引水，图即在沙漠中取水情形。

In rural areas, farmers make fires with tinder, and bellows are used to make the fire stronger. Here is the kitchen of a poor Mongolian family.

中国北方农家，广泛用柴草做燃料，在炉灶旁用风箱鼓风，增强火势。图为内蒙穷苦人家在炉灶旁拉风箱情形。

The large kitchen of a well-off family in the northern region of China.

中国北方殷实之家中的大灶台

Young women of the Li Nationality wear turbans, heavy necklaces and bracelets. According to local custom, a naked upper body is beautiful and healthy.

黎族少女以头缠包头布，项戴重重项圈，腕饰手镯，并上身裸露为美。图中的黎族少女给人以健康的青春美。

A dance for men of the Miao Nationality. Most Miao men can dance well while blowing reed pipes.

苗族的男子四人舞蹈。在苗族，男子能歌善舞，他们在吹奏竽笙的同时，伴着有节奏的舞蹈，招徕异性，往往成为节日间男女结交的方式。

During festivals, men and women of the Miao Nationality get to know and court each other at dances.

苗族女子在男子的竽笙伴奏下，翩翩起舞，不仅增加了节日气氛，同时也是男女恋爱的方式。

Wrestling is a favorite sport of the Mongolians. During festivals, men take part in wrestling competitions to show their strength.

在蒙古，摔跤是一项普遍开展的体育活动。往往在节日里举行男子的摔跤竞赛，以显示蒙古汉子的力量。

Chinese chess is a popular entertainment among men on the street, as well as the upper class.

下象棋是中国传统的消闲娱乐活动，同时也是一种智力的较量，在中国大江南北，贵族平民中，这项活动十分普遍。

Manchu children doing exercises.

清末做新式体操的满族儿童

People celebrate traditional festivals with the lion dance and land boat dance. Dancers in their holiday garb and wearing heavy makeup parade in the street to the rhythm of drums and gongs.

耍狮子与划旱船是中国传统节日期间活跃节日气氛的娱乐活动,表演者浓妆艳抹,按着节目和着音乐伴奏,边走边舞。

Before modern movies became popular in China, there were still picture shows. Viewers looked through a magnifying glass at pictures which were changed at regular intervals by pulling a rope. The pictures made up vivid stories as a narrator explained with song.

路旁看拉洋片。在现代电影未普及之前,中国民间有一种手绘画面,通过光线可见一种类似幻灯片的效果。并通过手拉动画面,形成不同画面组成的故事情节。拉洋片者,同时还要说唱,为画面配音。

In the northern region, rivers and lakes freeze in winter. Skating is a favorite sport among the northerners.

中国北方冬季,河湖结冰,成为自然的大冰场。每逢冬季,在冰上滑冰、乘冰车,成为北方冬季民间的娱乐和体育活动。

In old times, many families kept dogs to guard their houses. Noble families also kept dogs of fine breeds such as Pekinese and pugs as pets.

中国民间多有养狗看家的习惯,但是在旧中国上层官宦人家中也作为一种爱好和乐趣,或作为时髦,如贵妇人手牵哈叭狗之类。

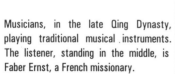

Musicians, in the late Qing Dynasty, playing traditional musical instruments. The listener, standing in the middle, is Faber Ernst, a French missionary.

清末华北一带的中国传统民族乐器表演,演奏的乐器有扬琴等。观看表演者为法国传教士法布尔·吉斯主教。

Prostitution, though looked upon as a corrupt practice, has thrived for a long time. Here is Rong'anli, a red-light district in Dandong.

卖淫是古老的陋习。图为丹东的妓院集中区荣安里。

Fengxian and Xiaogui, famous prostitutes in Beijing in the late Qing Dynasty.

清末北京名妓凤仙、小桂合影。

Hua Sibao, a famous prostitute in Shanghai in the 1910's.

清末民初沪妓花四宝

Xiangguochiren, a famous prostitute in
Beijing, in the late Qing Dynasty.

清末北京妓女香国痴人

Sai Jinhua, a famous prostitute in Beijing
in the late Qing Dynasty.

清末北京名妓赛金花

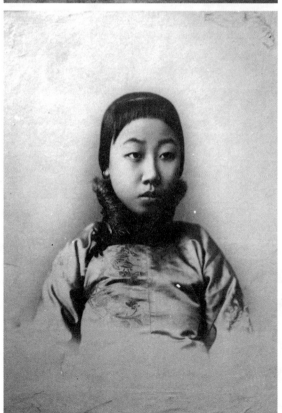

Yuxian, a famous prostitute in Beijing in
the late Qing Dynasty.

清末北京妓女玉仙

Li Pingxiang, a famous prostitute in
Beijing in the late Qing Dynasty.

清末北京妓女李苹香

Li Wenyun, a famous prostitute in Beijing in the early republican period.

民初北京妓女李文韵

Manchu prostitutes in Beijing in the late Qing Dynasty.

清末北京满族无名妓女

Han Prostitutes in Beijing toward the end of the Qing Dynasty.

清末北京汉族无名妓女

A prostitute and her Manchu patron, Beijing, in the late Qing Dynasty.

清末北京满族嫖客与妓女

A prostitute and her patron, Beijing, in the late Qing Dynasty.

清末北京嫖客与妓女

Tobacco was introduced to China in the Ming Dynasty. Here is an old man smoking with a water pipe made of bamboo in Yunnan in the republican period.

明代烟草就传入中国，各地吸食各有不同，图所反映的是民国时期云南一带用竹制的水烟筒吸烟的情形。

Gambling, has been in existence for a long time in China. Here is a gambling den in the Northeast of China in the republican era.

赌博是传统的陋习，历代均有，图为民国时期东北一带某赌场。

Opium was brought to China in the middle period of the Qing Dynasty. Many Chinese became opium addicts. Here is an opium den in the republican period.

清朝中叶鸦片流入中国，毒害甚巨。图为民国时期的某大烟馆。

In ancient China, small feet were considered beautiful and graceful. So women bound their feet when they were young and suffered greatly. Here, a woman is washing her deformed feet.

妇女缠足，是中国传统的残害妇女的陋习之一。女孩年幼时即用缠足布将足缠紧，限制脚的正常发育，形成骨骼变形的"小脚"，为此妇女要付出极大的痛苦。图为一妇女洗小脚的情形。

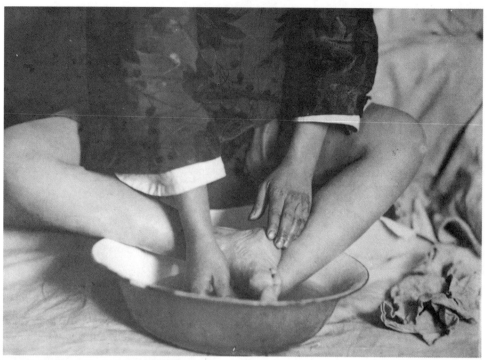

The so-called three-inch shoes.

三寸金莲鞋

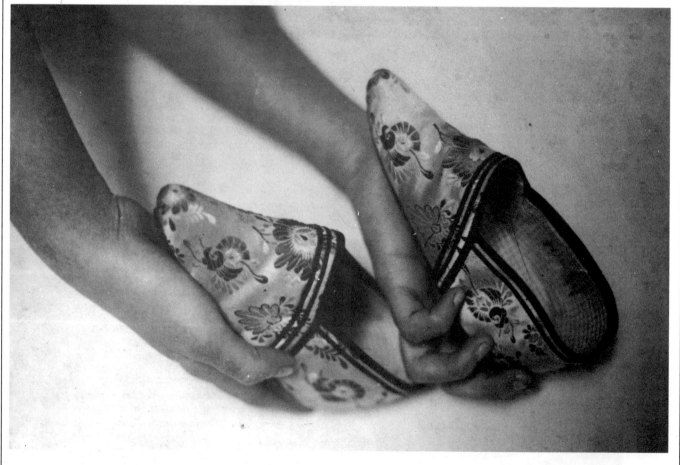

An old woman beggar. 乞丐老妇

A child begging on the street, Xi'an. 西安街头要饭的儿童

A junk collector. 捡破烂

文教卫生篇
CULTURE, EDUCATION AND MEDICINE

中国是几千年的文明古国,从来就对文化十分重视,其文化教育、体育、卫生等历史悠久,且自成体系,独具特色,在世界文明史中占有极其重要的位置。

伴随十九世纪中叶西方列强的殖民侵略,西方教育制度以及教育内容与形式、医疗体制以及医疗方法与技术、体育亦传入中国,给中国传统的封建式文教卫生模式以巨大的冲击与挑战,在激烈的冲突和互相的融合中,逐渐形成中西合璧的独特的旧中国文教卫生格局。

本篇精选五十余幅照片,反映旧中国的文教卫生状况,这些照片大致可分为以下几类:

有关教育:包括传统的官学(如国子监)、私学(如一些书院),以及与之相应的考试制度;西方人在中国开办的西式学堂;中国政府开办的新式学堂;还有各类职业教育、向国外派遣留学生等等。

有关医疗卫生:包括一些西方人在中国开办的西式医院,以及一些医疗卫生方面的事件等等。

有关体育和其它文化设施:包括一些近代体育场馆、图书馆、歌剧院等公众文化设施,以及与之相关的一些文体活动,特别是日伪时期,日本帝国文义借文体活动进行文化侵略所举办的各类展览、表演等等。

As one of the oldest civilizations on the planet, China, since ancient times, has placed great value on cultural affairs, especially the arts, education, sports, and medicine. The uniqueness of Chinese culture makes up an important contribution to the world civilization at large.

In the wake of Western battleships, Western sports, education and medicine were introduced to China, posing a great challenge to traditional Chinese institutions. A unique educational and medical system came into being in Old China as the result of a fusion between Chinese and Western ideas. This chapter, containing approximately fifty photographs, is divided into three parts: education, medicine, and sports.

Also included in the Culture, Education and Medicine Chapter are the exhibitions and performances organized by Japanese invaders in an attempt to conquer the Chinese people spiritually.

The Metropolitan College, the earliest of its kind in China, was founded in 1897. Here is a group photograph of teachers and students in 1910. Front row, fifth from left is Lao Naixuan, president of the college.

1897年筹办的京师大学堂是我国近代最早的大学。图为1910年京师大学堂师生合影。前排左起第五人为总监劳乃宣。

Students in the Chinese Department at Zhongxi Senior School, Jiangsu, during the late Qing Dynasty.

清末江苏高等中西学堂中文部学生合影

Students in the Mapping Department at Zhongxi Senior School, Jiangsu, toward the end of the Qing Dynasty.

清末江苏高等中西学堂测绘部学生合影

In 1906, Zhang Zhidong founded this primary school in Hubei. It was attached to the Lianghu Teachers' School. Here is a group photograph of its students.

1906年张之洞在原两湖书院旧址上办湖北两湖师范学堂附属小学,图为该校学生合影。

The School of Cheng'an County, Hebei.

河北成安县学堂

A group photograph of Chinese students and Chinese embassy personnel in New York City.

保定师范学堂建于清末,称直隶第二师范学堂(天津师范学堂称直隶第一师范),位于保定西关,1928年后改为河北省立第二师范。

Baoding Teachers' School, or the No. 2 Teachers' School of Hebei Province, was founded at Xiguan, Baoding, toward the end of the Qing Dynasty.

清代部分留美中国学生与使馆官员在纽约的合影

Cai Yuanpei and Jiang Guanyun founded a women's school in Shanghai in 1902. Here is a group photograph of its teachers and students.

1902年蔡元培和蒋观云等在上海创办爱国女学校。图为该校教职员与学生的合影。

The auditorium of Guangdong School in the late Qing Dynasty.

清末广东学堂礼堂

Teachers of the Peking Normal University held a farewell party for Li Xiangchen, president of the university, before his tour of the Western countries in 1923.

1923年北京师大同仁欢送前校长李湘宸赴欧美考察教育。

北京华北聋哑学校
Beijing North China
Deaf-Mute School.

The Japanese Guandong Engineering
Institute in the republican era.

民国时期日本关东工程学院

The first gathering of the Women's
Association of Self-Exertion and Practice
on May 17, 1911.

1911年5月17日，女子自振崇实会
初次游艺会。

A primary school in Inner Mongolia in the early Manchukuo period.

伪满初期内蒙的小学校

In 1902, the Qing government founded the Agricultural High School of Hebei Province in Baoding. Here students are learning how to sew seeds.

1902年清朝政府在保定建立直隶高等农学堂。图为该校学生实习春耕播种。

Students of the Animal Husbandry Department of Guizhou Provincial Forestry School in the late Qing Dynasty.

清朝末年贵州全省林学堂畜牧科学生开学合影

Teachers and the sixty students of the No. 4 Weaving Technique Institution in Zhuyi Village, Jizhou City, Hebei, 1914.

1914年河北冀州褚仪村冀四织工传习所教员与六十名学员合影

The Vocational Training Institution of Tianjin in the late Qing Dynasty.

清朝末年的天津习艺所

A primary school in a Japanese Immigrant Village during Manchukuo period.

伪满时期日本移民村内的小学校

A primary school in Taipei, while under the colonial rule of Japan.

日殖时期台北州下南澳童教育所

The Capital Library (present Beijing National Library) was founded in 1909. The library had been located in Zhihuasi Temple, Qingxiaolou and Jurentang successively. In 1931, it was moved to Wenjin Street. Here is the National Library while in Jurentang, Zhongnanhai, Beijing, in 1930.

清朝京师图书馆是现北京图书馆的前身,1909年建立。该馆先后以什刹海广化寺、北海庆霄楼、中南海居仁堂等地为馆址,1931年建成文津街新馆。图为1930年位于北京中南海居仁堂的国立图书馆外景。

The first conference of the China Library Association was held in Nanjing, January 28, 1929. Here is the group photograph of its participants at the opening ceremony.

1929年1月28日在南京召开中华图书馆协会第一次年会。图为会议代表在开幕典礼上的合影。

A group photograph of colleagues at the Peiping National Library in October 1930. Standing in the middle wearing glasses is Yuan Tongli, head of the library.

1930年10月,国立北平图书馆图书展览会同仁合影。中立戴眼镜者为当时国立北平图书馆长袁同礼。

The library of the North China Jushilin
Lay Buddhist Society, January 1941.

1941年1月的华北居士林图书馆

Tianjin Exhibition Hall for Educational
Articles toward the end of the Qing
Dynasty.

清朝末年的天津教育品陈列馆

The South Asian Trade Fair, jointly organized by the government and private citizens, was open to the public in Nanjing on June 5, 1910. This fair, lasting about six months, included several sections such as agriculture, art, medicine, machinery, and transportation. Here is the art exhibition hall.

1910年6月5日官商合办的南洋劝业会于南京开幕,内设农业、工艺、美术、医药、机械、通运等陈列馆,展览历时六个月。图为南洋劝业会中美术馆外景。

The Harbin Museum in the republican period.

民国时期哈尔滨的大博物馆

The Chinese Exhibition Hall at the Paris Trade Fair, 1900.

1900年巴黎博览会上的中国馆

Guozijian, the National University, in 1901, when Beijing was captured by the allied forces.

1901年八国联军占领北京期间的国子监辟雍。院落内冷冷清清,杂草丛生,一片凄凉景象。

The Bailu Academy, established in the Song Dynasty, is located at the foot of the Wulao Peak, Lushan Mountain, Jiangxi. It is one of the most influential private schools in the history of China.

白鹿书院。位于江西星子县庐山五老峰下,始建于宋代,是中国古代书院中影响最大的一座。

In the Qing Dynasty, civil service examinations were held in a place called the Gongyuan. Candidates who passed local examinations became known as "Juren". Here is the Qinhuai Gongyuan, Nanjing. It contains approximately one hundred rows of houses; each row contains up to a hundred cabins. During the examination, every candidate is numbered and locked into his own cabin to prevent cheating.

贡院是清代科举制度中举行乡试的场所,考中者称举人。图为清朝的南京秦淮贡院。考场内数十间甚至百余间为一列,多达百余列,形如长巷。应试者按编号进入,参加考试,相互隔绝,以防作弊。

The first national conference of the China Association for the Promotion of Kwoyeu Romatzyh was held in Zhengzhou on Sept. 24, 1934. More than 70 scholars participated in the conference which was presided over by Li Jinxi. This association played an important role in promoting the correct usage of phonetic symbols in China.

中华民国国语罗马字促进会为改革汉字,于1934年9月24日在郑州举行第一次全国代表大会,会议代表七十余人,大会主席为黎锦熙,会议为中国汉字实现拼音化,统一国语起了重要作用。图为大会闭幕时的会场。

Members of the Chengnan Poetry Society, 1940. 城南诗社同仁1940年留影

Members of the Chengnan Poetry Society, 1937. 1937年正月城南诗社同仁合影

The Jinling Buddhist Scriptures (Xylographical) Publishing House was started by Yang Wenhui in 1866. The publishing house, which produced the most Buddhist Scriptures in modern times, has made great contributions to preserving and spreading Chinese Buddhist culture. In 1911, Yang died. His apprentice, Ouyang Jingwu, carried forward his work and founded a research department for sutra publication in March 1915. Here are members of the research department (front row, left to right): Huang Zishan, Liu Baoyi, Wang Shaohu. Back row: Lu Qiuyi, Wu Aiping, Ouyang Jingwu, Huang Jihua, and Yao Bainian.

1866年杨文会建金陵刻经处于南京，是中国近代持续时间最长、刻印佛教经卷最多的刻经处，对保护和弘扬中国佛教经藏具有重大贡献。1911年杨文会去世后，弟子欧阳竞无继承延续至今。此为1915年3月金陵刻经处研究部成员合影。前排左起黄了山、刘抱一、王少湖；后排左起吕秋一、邬爱平、欧阳竞无、黄悸华、姚柏年。

In 1881, Li Hongzhang founded the Northern Hospital. Later, it was renamed Northern Medical College.

1881年李鸿章创办的北洋施医院，后改称北洋医学堂。

Around 1911, a plague broke out in Northeast China and soon spread to Hebei and Shandong provinces. The Qing government ordered local officials to take immediate measures to wipe out the epidemic. At the same time, the International Symposium on Plague was held in Fengtian on April 3. Experts from eleven countries participated in the symposium, which was presided over by Wu Liande, the chief medical officer of Northeast China. Here is a group photograph of the participants.

1911年前后，东三省发生鼠疫，并蔓延直鲁两省，清朝政府一面命民政部及地方督抚迅速扑灭，同时于是年4月3日在奉天省城召开万国鼠疫研究会，十一国代表与会，由中国东三省总医官伍连德主持。图为与会代表的合影。

A Japanese Red Cross hospital, Lushun. 旅顺日本红十字医院

A group photograph of the staff of Minnan Hospital with Chen Zhaoying, a member of the Central Executive Committee of the Kuomintang on March 19, 1931.

1931年3月19日闽南医院全体人员欢迎中委陈肇英等人的合影。

Hankou Race Track during the republican period.

民国时期的汉口洋人竞马场

Located at Dongsipailou, Peiping Municipal Hospital was founded in 1905. At that time, it mainly offered medical services to Germans. After World War II, it was renamed Peiping Hospital. Here is the hospital in 1946.

北平市立医院始建于1905年,原为德国医院,位于东单牌楼,主要为在华德国人服务。第二次世界大战胜利后,改为北平医院。图为1946年改名后的医院大门。

A clinic in Mongolia. 蒙古的医疗所门面

China Red Cross, Peiping Hospital, 1946.
1946年的中国红十字会北平医院大门

Peiping French Hospital at Dongjiao-minxiang, 1946.

北平法国医院位于北京东交民巷。图为1946年的该院大门。

Peiping Tongren Hospital was established by the American Methodist Church in 1886. At first, it was located in Xiaoshun Lane, Chongwenmen. In 1903, it was moved to Dongjiaominxiang. Here is the hospital in 1946.

北平美国同仁医院始建于1886年，由美国美以美会创办，原址北京崇文门孝顺胡同，1903年后改建于东郊民巷东口。图为1946年该院大门。

Peiping Municipal Psychiatric Hospital, 1946.

1946年北平市立精神病疗养院的大门

A wrestling match, Mongolia.

蒙古祭典后力拔比赛——摔跤

A swimming pool in the Nanjing Central Stadium in the republican period.

民国时期的南京中央体育场游泳池

The National Race Track in Changchun in the Manchukuo period.

伪满时期长春的国立赛马场

The opening ceremony of the North China City Games, which was sponsored by the Japanese-controlled North China Government Administrative Commission.

由伪华北政务委员会组织的"华北都市友好运动会"开幕式情形。

The North China City Games.

伪华北都市友好运动会组团仪式

The main stadium for the North China City Games, Qingdao City.

伪华北都市友好运动会运动场外景(青岛)。

The Japanese sumo performance at the North China City Games.

伪华北政务委员会邀请的日本相扑表演

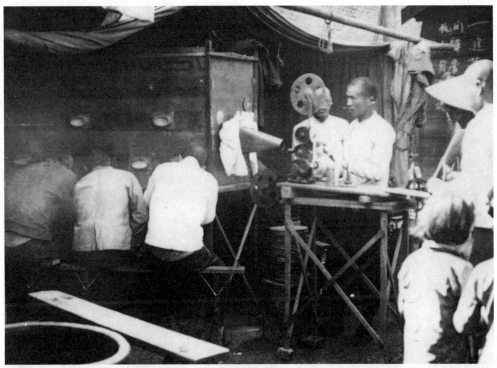

A projection room on the street in the republican period.

民国时期的街头放映馆

A storytelling house in "South Manchu-kuo", while under the Japanese rule.

日伪时期"南满"的说唱馆

人物篇 PERSONALITIES

　　旧中国一直处在激烈动荡之中,先是最后一个封建王朝被推翻,又有民国初年政府的频频更迭,各路军阀为抢地盘互相混战;日本侵华战争爆发后,又有卖国投敌的汉奸成立伪政府……一时混乱不堪,出现了众多政治、军事、外交等方面风云一时的人物,"生旦净末丑",在历史这座大舞台上,真可谓"你唱罢来我登场","各领风骚数年间"。

　　本篇收录了近百幅人物照片,主要是一些活动在旧中国政治、军事、外交舞台上的反面人物,包括晚清的皇帝、王爷、贝勒、皇族成员、各部堂官和掌握实权的封疆大吏;民国初年的总统、总理、各部部长、次长、驻外使节、地方督军和省长、拥兵割据一方的军阀;日本侵华战争期间的伪政府主席、委员长、伪政府要员;等等。

　　这些人物当中,窃国大盗有之,玩弄权术的野心家有之,谄上欺下的政治掮客有之,卖国求荣的汉奸败类有之,几度沉浮官场而怏怏不乐者有之;或主角,或配角,都在旧中国这出阴暗、悲怆的大戏中扮演了不同的角色。

Old China's history is a turbulent one. The fall of the last feudal empire was followed by a series of chaotic events: frequently reconstructed early republican governments, warfare among China's many warlords, Japan's full-scale invasion, and the establishment of a Japanese-controlled puppet government. Along with these various upheavals, the responsible historical figures, admirable or despicable, shifted as often as if they were on a merry-go-round. A hundred or so of these historical figures are introduced in the Personalities Chapter. Most of them played negative roles in the history of Old China in fields of politics, military and foreign affairs.

Pu Yi (1906 — 1967), the last emperor of the Qing Dynasty. This picture was taken in 1931.

溥仪(1906 1967),爱新觉罗氏,字浩然,满洲正黄旗人。此照系其着军服摄于1931年。

曾国荃(1824—1890),字沅甫,号叔纯,湖南湘乡人。曾任两广总督、两江总督。

Chong Hou (1826 — 1893), Manchu, official in charge of the trade in Tianjin, Niu-zhuang and Yantai ports, and deputy governor-general of Zhili (present-day Hebei).

崇厚(1826—1893),完颜氏,字地山,满洲镶黄旗人。曾任三口通商大臣,署直隶总督,后因擅自签订中俄《里瓦几亚条约》被革职下狱,后获释。

Zeng Guoquan (1824 — 1890), born in Xiangxiang, Hunan. Governor-general of Guangdong-Guangxi provinces and governor-general of Liangjiang, an area covering present-day Jiangsu, Anhui and Jiangxi.

Zeng Jize (1839-1890), born in Xiangxiang, Hunan. Envoy to England, France, and Russia. Vice minister of war and part-time official of the Ministry of Foreign Affairs. He signed the Sino-Russian Ili Treaty on China's behalf.

曾纪泽(1839—1890),字刚,湖南湘乡人。曾任驻英、法、俄大臣,兵部左侍郎兼总理衙门行走。曾主持交涉索还伊犁事宜,签订《中俄伊犁条约》。

Bao Jun (? — 1891), Manchu. A member of the Privy Council, foreign minister and minister of the Board of War.

宝鋆(?—1891),索绰络氏,字佩蘅,满州镶白旗人。曾任军机大臣,总理各国事务大臣,兵部尚书。

Yi Xin (1832 — 1898), Manchu. Younger brother of Emperor Xianfeng, and Prince of Gong. War minister and foreign minister during the reigns of Tongzhi and Guangxu emperors.

奕䜣(1832—1898)，爱新觉罗氏，咸丰皇帝的异母弟，恭亲王。曾任军机大臣及总理衙门大臣，主持同治、光绪两朝的外交事务。

Zhang Yinyuan (1837 — 1900) born in Nanhai, Guangdong. Vice minister of Finance, and envoy to the United States. He was executed by Empress Dowager Cixi in 1900.

张荫垣(1837—1900)，字樵野，广东南海人。曾任户部左侍郎，出使美国大臣。1900年被慈禧太后处死。

Tan Sitong (1865 — 1898) born in Liuyang, Hunan. A late Qing Dynasty progressive who tried in vain to introduce political reform in China. Tan was executed by Empress Dowager Cixi following the failure of the Coup of Wuxu in 1898.

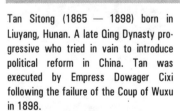

谭嗣同(1865—1898)，字复生，号壮飞，湖南浏阳人。1898年戊戌变法中的激进派人士，参与新政。戊戌变法失败后，被捕就义，是"戊戌六君子"之一。

Xu Jingcheng (1845 — 1900) born in Jiaxing, Zhejiang. Envoy to Russia, foreign minister and vice minister of Public Works. He spared no effort to suppress the Boxer Uprising and later was executed by Empress Dowager Cixi in 1900.

许景澄(1845—1900)，原名癸身，字竹筠，浙江嘉兴人。曾任驻俄公使，总理衙门大臣，兼工部左侍郎。1900年力主镇压义和团。后被慈禧太后下令处死。

Yuan Xu (1846—1900) born in Tonglu, Zhejiang. Official in charge of worships and sacrifices, low-ranking official in the Board of Finance and secretariat official in the Ministry of Foreign Affairs.

袁昶 (1846—1900)，原名振蟾，字爽秋，一字重黎，浙江桐庐人。曾任太常寺卿，户部主事，总理衙门章京。1900年力主镇压义和团。后被慈禧太后下令处死。此照为袁昶1899年所摄。

Li Hongzhang (1823—1901) born in Hefei, Anhui. Governor-general of Zhili, Wenhuadian Scholar. Li rose to prominence in the 1860s as organizer and commander of the Anhui (Huai) Army, a major in quelling the Taiping Revolution (1851-1864). Later he became a key role in the Self-Strengthening Program. During the late Qing Dynasty, he was the country's most important negotiator and signed a series of traitorous treaties such as the Treaty of Shimonoseki with Japan in 1895, and the Peace Treaty of 1901.

李鸿章 (1823—1901)，字少荃，安徽合肥人。曾任直隶总督，兼北洋大臣，文华殿大学士。早年创办淮军镇压太平天国，后兴办洋务，长期操纵清朝政府的政治、军事、外交。曾主持签订中日《马关条约》、《辛丑条约》等一系列重大卖国条约。

Yu Geng (? — 1902), an official in the Ministry of Foreign Affairs and an envoy to France.

裕庚 (?—1902)，字朗西，汉军正白旗人。曾任总理衙门大臣、出使法国大臣。

Song Qing (1820—1902) born in Penglai, Shandong. He was removed from office following the defeat in the Sino-Japanese War (1894 — 1895). Later he was commissioned to help establish the Beiyang Army.

宋庆 (1820—1902)，字祝三，山东蓬莱人。中日甲午战争爆发后，任前方各军统领，因战事失利被革职留任，后曾协办北洋军务。

Liu Kunyi (1830—1902) born in Xinning, Hunan. Official in Charge of civil and financial administration in Guangxi Province, governor of Guangdong-Guangxi provinces, then Liangjiang Province and Nanyang trade minister. During the early years of his career, he joined the Hunan (Xiang) Army to suppress the Taiping Revolution, later advocated the Self-Strengthening Program.

刘坤一(1830—1902),字岘庄,湖南新宁人。曾任广西布政使,江西巡抚,两广总督,两江总督兼南洋通商大臣。早年入湘军参与镇压太平天国运动,后参与洋务运动,1900年义和团运动时,与张之洞等人同洋人勾结宣布"东南护保",之后倡办"回銮新政"。

Tao Mo (1835 — 1902, seated) born in Jiaxing, Zhejiang. Governor of Xijiang Province, and governor-general of Guangdong-Guangxi provinces.

Rong Lu (1836 — 1904), Manchu. Governor-general of Zhili Province, and war minister. In 1898, he helped the Empress Dowager Cixi suppress the reform movement. In 1900, he was ordered by Cixi to make a feign attack to the Legation Quarter in an attempt to protect westerners during the Boxer Uprising.

荣禄(1836—1904),瓜尔佳氏,字仲华,满洲正白旗人。曾任直隶总督,军机大臣。1898年协助慈禧太后发动"戊戌政变",镇压维新运动;1900年奉慈禧之命,围攻北京使馆区,暗中保护洋人,之后随慈禧逃往西安。

陶模(1835—1902),字方之,浙江嘉兴人。曾任西疆巡抚,两广总督。坐者为陶模。

Huang Zunxian (1848 — 1905) born in Meixian County, Guangdong. Councilor in Japan. Later Huang went to San Francisco as Chinese Consul-general. During the Coup of Wuxu, he was impeached and then resigned.

黄遵宪(1848—1905),字公度,别号境庐主人,广东梅县人。曾任驻日本公使馆参赞,驻美国旧金山总领事。"戊戌政变"时,因参与维新运动遭弹劾,后回乡闲居。

Yang Shixiang (1858 — 1908) born in Sixian County, Anhui. Governer-General of Zhili Province.

杨士骧(1858—1908),字萍石,安徽泗县人。曾任直隶总督。

Wang Wenshao (1839-1908) born in Hangzhou, Zhejiang. Governor-general of Zhili Province, war minister, and government administration councilor. Wang had a hand in quelling the Taiping Revolution. Later he advocated the Westernization Movement and leaned toward the reformers during the Coup of Wuxu.

王文韶(1839—1908),字夔石,号耕娱,浙江杭州人。曾任直隶总督,军机大臣,政务处大臣。早年镇压太平天国运动,后参与洋务运动。1898年"戊戌变法"时倾向维新。1900年随慈禧逃往西安,参与"回銮新政"。

Zhang Zhidong (1837—1909) a native of Nanpi, Hebei. Governor-general of Huguang, War Minister, and Tirenge Scholar. Zhang was a champion of hard-line resistance in the Sino-French War in 1884. Later he became a leading advocate and practitioner of the Self-Strengthening Modernization Program and set up a number of western-style enterprises such as the Hubei Gun Factory and the Kaiping Mining Administration.

张之洞(1837—1909),字孝达,号香涛,晚号抱冰,直隶(今河北)南皮人。曾任湖广总督,体仁阁大学士,军机大臣。1884年主持两广抵抗法国侵略军的战争,是中法战争的主战派核心人物。战后大办洋务企业,创办湖北枪炮厂、开平矿务局等。1895年反对签订中日《马关条约》。1900年与外国势力勾结,宣布东南护保。反对维新变法,参与"回銮新政"。

Dai Hongci (? — 1910) born in Nanhai, Guangdong. Government Compiler, Minister of Justice and War Minister.
Front row left to right: Dai Hongci and Yuan Shikai.
Back row: Pu Lun, Tang Shaoyi, (?), and Sun Baoqi.

戴鸿慈(?—1910),字少怀,广东南海人。授编修,刑部尚书,军机大臣。
前排左起:端方、戴鸿慈、袁世凯。
后排左起:溥伦、唐绍仪、×××、孙宝琦。

Ting Jie (? — 1910), Manchu. Deputy Shengjing General, and Minister of Justice.

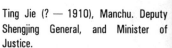

廷杰(?—1910),满洲正蓝旗人。曾任署盛京将军,后任法部尚书。

Robert Martv (1835 — 1911) born in Northern Ireland. Inspector General of Customs in China.

赫德 *Robert Martv*
(1835—1911),字鹭宾,英国人,生于北爱尔兰。曾任中国海关总税务司。此照摄于1908年赫德回国后。

Song Shou (?—1911), Manchu. Minister of Public Works, Governor-general of Chahar, and Fujian-Zhejiang provinces. In Nov. 1911, Song committed suicide by swallowing gold.

松寿(?—1911),字鹤龄,满洲正白旗人。曾任工部尚书,察哈尔都统,闽浙总督。1911年11月吞金自杀。本照为其六十岁所摄。

Duan Fang (1861 — 1911), Manchu. Governor-general of Zhili, official in charge of the construction of the Chuanhan and Yuehan Railroads. He was killed during the Revolution of 1911.

端方(1861—1911),托忒克氏,字午桥,号匋斋,满洲正白旗人。曾任直隶总督,被免职后又被启用为川汉、粤汉铁路大臣。辛亥革命中被起义军所杀。

Chen Baochen (1852 — ?, left) born in Minhuo, Fujian. Tutor of Emperor Pu Yi, and Bidege Consultant. During Zhang Xun's restoration of the Qing emperor, Chen was commissioned as a cabinet member. To his right is Zhang Renjun.

陈宝琛(1852—?),字伯潜,福建闽侯人,曾是溥仪的师傅,并任弼德院顾问大臣。参与张勋复辟,任内阁议政大臣。图左立者为陈宝琛,右立者为张人骏。

Duan Xun, Manchu. Governor of Hovd.

端洵,字景苏,满洲正黄旗人。曾任科布多参赞大臣并总署大臣。

Lian Fang, Jinzhou General. He paid a visit to the Western countries in the Burlingame Diplomatic Corps in 1868.

联芳,字春卿,汉镶白旗人。曾任荆州将军。1868年曾随蒲安臣使团出访欧美,是清朝政府培养的第一代洋务人才。

Yang Shu, an alternate magistrate of Guangdong Province and a counselor in the Ministry of Foreign Affairs.

杨枢,字星垣,汉军正黄旗人。曾任广东候补道,外务部左参议。

The six Qing Beizi (a rank of Manchu nobility below that of prince).

1906年(清光绪三十二年)科尔沁贝子、敖汉贝子与巴林贝子等六人结盟时合影。

Pang Hongshu, a native of Changshu, Jiangsu. Governor of Guizhou Province.

庞鸿书,江苏常熟人。曾任贵州巡抚。

Bao Fen, Mongolian. Governor of Henan, and Shanxi. He had a hand in quelling the Revolution of 1911, and lived in seclusion during the republican era.

宝棻,字湘石,蒙古正蓝旗人。曾任河南巡按， 山西巡按等。1911年参与镇压河南革命党人。民国后隐居。

Rong Xun (1870 — ?), Manchu. Vice minister of tribal affairs.

荣勋(1870—?),字竹农,满洲正白旗人。曾任理蕃院左侍郎。

Yin Chang, Manchu. As an army general, he took part in suppressing the Revolution of 1911. During the republican era, he was commissioned as a general, and chief of the general staff.

Zhang Renjun, born in Fengrun, Hebei. Governor-general of Liangjiang, and then Guangdong-Guangxi provinces.

张人骏,字千里,又字安圃,河北丰润人。曾任两江、两广总督。此照摄于两广总督任所。

荫昌,字午楼,满洲正白旗人。曾任陆军大臣,军咨大臣。1911年曾率清军南下镇压武昌起义。民国建立后,曾任陆军上将、参谋总长、参议员、参议等职。

Na Yantu, a Mongolian prince, Uliastai General, and vice chairman of the Senate during the republican era.

那彦图,字距甫,蒙古镶黄旗人。世袭蒙古旗喀尔喀萨亲王,曾任牙里雅苏台将军。民国时曾任参议院副议长。

Na Tong, Manchu. Foreign minister, Tirenge Scholar and Bideyuan Counselor in Yuan Shikai's Cabinet. He took part in the peace talks with the allied forces in 1900. He lived in seclusion in Tianjin during the republican era.

那桐,叶赫那拉氏,字琴轩,满洲镶黄旗人。曾任总理衙门大臣,体仁阁大学士。1900年随奕劻、李鸿章参与八国联军议和。1911年曾任袁世凯内阁弼德院顾问大臣。民国后隐居天津。

Gui Chun, Manchu. Official in charge of the storage of rice transported to the capital city by water as farm tax, and official of civil affairs.

桂春,字月亭,满洲正蓝旗人。曾任仓场侍郎、民政大臣。此照为其任仓场侍郎时所摄。

Three sons of Yi Xuan, 1902. Left to right: Zai Tao, Zai Feng (father of Xuantong Emperor) and Zai Xun.

醇亲王奕譞三子合影。左起载涛、载沣(宣统皇帝溥仪之父)、载洵。此照为载沣20岁时(1902年)所摄。

Front row left to right: Liu Ruozeng, Jiang Han, Wang Kaiyun, Wang Shudan, and Hu Yujin. Back row: Chang Yi, Cao Jingrun, Zeng Guangjun, Chen Zhaokui, Yang Zongji, Liu Yi and Zheng Yuan.

王闿运、江瀚等人合影。前排自左至右:刘若曾、江瀚、王闿运、王树枏、胡玉缙。后排自左至右:常怡、曹经沅、曾广钧、陈兆奎、杨宗稷、刘巽、郑沅。

En Shou (left), Manchu. Governor of Jiangsu, and then Shaanxi. Right is Bao Fen.

恩寿,索卓罗氏,字艺棠,满洲镶白旗人。曾任江苏巡抚,陕西巡抚。图左为恩寿,右为宝棻。

Wu Tingfang (1842 — 1922) born in Xinhui, Guangdong. Chinese ambassador to the United States, Spain, and Peru. Foreign minister, and acting prime minister in the Duan Qirui government.

伍廷芳(1842—1922),字文爵,号秩庸,广东新会人。历任驻美国、西班牙、秘鲁公使。任段祺瑞政府外交总长、代理总理、军政府外交部长并曾代行总统职。此照为其1896年出任驻美国大使时所摄。

Lu Huaihuan, minister of the Board of War, foreign minister, and official to supervise the construction of the Jinpu Railroad.

吕海环,曾任江南常镇通海道、兵部尚书、外务部尚书、督办津浦铁路大臣。

Shi Zhao (1877 — ?) born in Hangxian County, Zhejing. Chinese ambassador to the United States, and a senator during the republican era.

施肇(1877—?),字植之,浙江杭县人。曾任驻美大使、国民参政员等职。此照摄于1909年。

Huang Xing (1864 — 1916) born in Changsha, Hunan. A leader of the 1911 republican revolution. In 1905, he joined Sun Yet-sen to found the Tong Meng Hui, in which he was renowned as an organizer and military strategist. He was minister of war in the provisional government of Nanjing and joined the opposition to Yuan Shikai in 1913.

黄兴（1864—1916），原名轸，字廑午，湖南长沙人。曾与孙中山先生共建同盟会，武昌起义后任革命军总司令，在南京临时政府中任陆军参谋总长。

Zhi Rui (1852 — 1912), Manchu. General of Hangzhou, and Ili. He was killed in Xinjiang after the Revolution of 1911.

志锐（1852—1912），他他拉氏，字伯愚，满洲镶红旗人。曾任杭州、伊犁将军。辛亥革命后，为新疆起义新军所杀。

Yuan Shikai (1859 — 1916) born in Xiangcheng, Henan. Governor-general of Zhili, war minister, prime minister, and president after the establishment of the Republic of China. Proclaimed himself emperor in December 1915 and forced to abdicate the following year.

袁世凯（1859—1916），字慰亭，河南项城人。曾任直隶总督、军机大臣、内阁总理大臣。民国后任临时大总统，在北京建立北洋军阀政府，1915年12月复辟帝制，翌年被迫宣布取消帝制。

Xi Liang (1852 — 1917), Mongolian. Governor-general of Sichuan, Yunnan-Guizhou, and Jehol provinces.

锡良 (1852—1917),巴岳持氏,字清弼,蒙古镶蓝旗人。曾任四川总督,后任云贵总督,热河都统。

Zeng Qi (? — 1919), Manchu. Shengjing General and Guangzhou General. Signed a territory treaty with Russia without authorization in 1900.

增祺 (?—1919)伊拉里氏,字瑞堂,满洲镶白旗人。曾任盛京将军、广州将军等职。曾经于1900年擅自与俄国签定《奉天交地暂且章程》。此照摄于1909年。

Yi Kuang (1836 — 1918), Manchu, great-grand son of Emperor Qianlong. Prince of Qing, prime minister, and war minister. He signed the Peace Treat of 1901 with the allied forces and lived in seclusion in Tianjin during the republican era.

奕劻 (1836—1918),爱新觉罗氏,乾隆帝重孙,满洲镶蓝旗人。晋封庆亲王,曾任总理大臣、军机大臣。1900年同李鸿章主持与八国联军议和,次年签订《辛丑条约》。民国后避居天津。

Zheng Xiaoxu (1860 — 1938) born in Fuzhou, Fujian. Secretariat official in the Ministry of Foreign Affairs in the late Qing Dynasty. Premier and minister of culture and education in Manchukuo.

郑孝胥(1860—1938),字苏戡,号太夷,福州人。清朝总理衙门章京。伪"满洲国"成立以后,出任国务总理兼文教部总长。

Feng Guozhang (1857 — 1919) born in Hebei. Vice president and acting president in the Northern Warlords government. He joined Yuan Shikai and helped establish a Western-style army. As head of the Zhili clique of the Northern Warlords, he took part in quelling the 1911 republican revolution, and the Second Revolution against Yuan Shikai, but he opposed Yuan's enthronement.

冯国璋(1857—1919),字华甫,河北人。曾任北洋军阀政府副总统,代理总统。早年随袁世凯创办新建陆军,与王士珍、段祺瑞并称"北洋三杰",曾参与镇压辛亥革命、"二次革命";但曾反对袁世凯称帝。此照为冯国璋1917年代理北洋政府总统时所摄。

Liang Dingfen (1859 — 1919) born in Panyu, a provincial chief prosecutor, and provincial official in charge of both civil and financial administration.

梁鼎芬(1859—1919),字星海,号节庵,广东番禺人。曾任按察史。布政使等。

Li Jingfang (1855 — 1934) born in Hefei, Anhui, son of Li Hongzhang, envoy to Japan and Britain, and took part in talks following the Sino-Japanese War of 1894.

李经方(1855—1934),字伯行,安徽合肥人。曾任出使日本、英国大臣。随父李鸿章参与甲午中日议和谈判、《中俄密约》谈判。

Shan Qi (1866 — 1922), Manchu, the Prince of Su, minister of civil affairs, and minister of tribal affairs in the late Qing Dynasty.

善耆(1866—1922),字艾堂,满洲镶白旗人。承袭肃亲王,曾任民政大臣,理藩大臣。

Sun Yue (1878 — 1928) born in Gaoyang, Hebei, commander of the No.1 Northern Expeditionary Army, a member of the Tong Meng Hui, an officer in the Kuomintang National Military Council. He took part in both the Second Revolution, and the Beijing Coup in 1924.

孙岳(1878—1928),字禹行,河北高阳人。曾任北伐第一军司令,国民政府军委委员。早年加入同盟会,曾参加"二次革命",1924年与冯玉祥等发动"北京政变"。此照摄于1925年2月。

唐继尧(1882—1927),字蓂赓,云南会泽人。曾任云南都督。早年参加同盟会,辛亥革命时,随蔡锷发动昆明起义。1915年与蔡锷等通电反对袁世凯称帝。1917年参加护法运动,暗中勾结北洋军阀,排挤孙中山先生。

Tang Jiyao (1882 — 1927) born in Huize, Yunnan, a member of the Tong Meng Hui. He joined Cai E and launched the Kunming Uprising during the 1911 Revolution and took part in the military uprising against Yuan Shikai in 1915. During the movement to defend the Constitution in 1917, Tang, together with the Northern Warlords, squeeze out Dr. Sun Yet-sen.

Zhang Shaozeng (1880 — 1928) born in Dacheng, Hebei, chief military training inspector in the Northern Army; commander-in-chief of the army and premier.

张绍曾(1880—1928),字敬舆,河北大城人。曾任北洋政府陆军训练总监、陆军部总长、国务总理。

Cao Rulin (1877—1966) a native of Shanghai, vice foreign minister in the late Qing Dynasty, minister of traffic and communications in the Northern Warlord government, and the supreme consultant in the puppet North China Provisional Government.

曹汝霖(1877—1966),字润田,上海人。先后任清外务部副大臣、北洋军阀政府交通总长、伪华北临时政府最高顾问。

Qi Xieyuan (1879—1946) born in Tianjin, civil administrative chief of Jiangsu, Anhui and Hubei provinces, and a member in the puppet North China Government Administrative Commission.

齐燮元(1879—1946),字抚万,天津市人。曾任苏、皖、赣巡阅使,伪华北政务委员会委员兼治安署督办。

Sa Zhenbing born in Minhou, Fujian, commander-in-chief of Guangdong Navy in the late Qing Dynasty, and governor of Fujian Province during the republican period.

萨镇冰(1859—1952),字鼎铭,福建闽侯人。曾任广东水师提督。民国时任福建省省长。

Tie Liang (1863 — 1938), Manchu, war minister, and Jiangning General.

铁良(1863—1938),字宝臣,满洲镶白旗人。曾任军机大臣,后调任江宁将军。

Lu Zhengxiang, (1871 — 1949) born in Shanghai, foreign minister in the Northern Warlords government.

陆征祥 (1871—1949)，亦名增祥，字子兴，上海市人。曾任北洋政府外交总长。

Wang Baorong (1878 — 1933), born in Wuxian, Jiangsu, a famous calligrapher, a member of the consultative council, constitution committee, and house of representatives.

汪荣宝 (1878—1933)，衮甫，号思玄，江苏吴县人。曾任资政院议员、协纂宪法大臣、众议院议员。擅书法，著有《清史讲义》等。

Duan Qirui (1865 — 1936) born in Hefei, Anhui. As one of the Yuan Shikai's chief subordinates in the Beiyang Army, he was Jiangbei Commander-in-chief, governor-general of Henan Province, and prime minister. In 1912, he published an open telegraph to force the abdication of the Qing Emperor. In 1917, he crushed Zhang Xun's attempt to restore the Qing Emperor. Duan also headed the Anhui Faction of warlords in rivalry with the Zhili clique under Feng Guozhang. That rivalry led to the Anhui-Zhili War in 1920. In 1924, he became the provisional president.

Liang Shiyi (1869 — 1933) born in Sanshui, Guangdong. This picture was taken in 1920 when he was minister of traffic and communications and chairman of the financial committee to deal with the affairs in the aftermath of the Duan Qirui government.

梁士诒 (1869—1933)，字翼夫，号燕孙，广东三水人。此照为1920年任段祺瑞政府财政善后委员会委员长兼交通银行总理时所摄。

段祺瑞 (1865—1936)，原名启瑞，字芝泉，安徽合肥人。历任北洋军械局委员、江北提督、河南督军、国务总理兼陆军总长等职。早年随袁世凯创办新建陆军，为北洋军阀皖系的首领。1912年曾通电迫使清帝逊位。1917年与黎元洪不和发生府院之争，后马厂誓师，粉碎张勋复辟。对德宣战后，任参战军督办。1920年直皖战争中失败辞职。1924年任临时执政。

Li Yuanhong (1864 — 1928) born in Huangpi, Hubei, vice president of the Nanjing provisional government, then president following the death of Yuan Shikai. As president, Li quarreled with militarists and tried to maneuver between factions but never acquired the authority to control policy effectively.

黎元洪(1864—1928),字宋卿,湖北黄陂人。曾任南京临时政府副总统。袁世凯死后,继任大总统。1917年与国务总理段祺瑞发生府院之争,被张勋驱走。

Cen Chunxuan (1861 — 1933) born in Xilin, Guangxi, governor-general of Sichuan Province, and Guangdong-Guangxi provinces. During the early republican era, he was commissioned as chairman of the Guangdong Military Government to defend the Constitution.

岑春煊(1861—1933),原名春泽,字云阶,广西西林人。曾任四川总督、两广总督。民国初任广东护法军政府主席总裁。

Duan Zhigui (1869 — 1925) born in Hefei, Anhui, commander-in-chief of the capital city, governor-general of Chahar Province and a general of the army.

段芝贵(1869—1925),字香严,安徽合肥人。民国时期,曾任驻京总司令、察哈尔都统,陆军上将。

Chimen Kalon, the most powerful among the four lay ministers (known as Kalons) in Tibet. He and Hsiacha Kalon had engaged in British-Tibetan affairs for more than 20 years.

持门加伦,持门为西藏四大加伦中最有权势者,持门加伦曾随虾札加伦办理英藏交涉二十余年。

胡惟德(1863—1933),字馨吾,浙江吴兴人。清驻俄大臣,外务部副大臣,民国后任唐绍仪内阁外交总长。

Hu Weide (1863 — 1933) born in Wuxing, Zhejiang. Minister to Russia, vice minister of foreign affairs in the late Qing Dynasty, and minister of foreign affairs in the Tang Shaoyi's Cabinet in the republican period.

Wei Lihuang (1896 — 1960) a native of Hefei, Anhui, a commander-in-chief during the Anti-Japanese War.

卫立煌(1896—1960),字俊如,安徽合肥人。抗战时期先后任第二战区副司令长官兼前敌总指挥及第一战区司令长官。

Sun Baoqi (1867 — 1931) born in Hangzhou, Zhejiang, governor of Shandong, minister of finance in the Northern Warlords government, premire and foreign minister of the Beijing Government.

孙宝琦(1867—1931),字慕韩,浙江杭州人。曾任山东巡抚,北洋政府财政总长,北京政府国务总理兼外交委员会委员长。此照摄于1915年。

陈箓(1877—1939),字任先,号止室,福建闽侯人。任伪维新政府外交部长。

Chen Lu (1877 — 1939) born in Minhou, Fujian, foreign minister in the puppet government.

Zai Feng (1883—1951), Manchu. During the late Qing Dynasty, he ruled as a prince regent.

载沣(1883—1951),爱新觉罗氏,号伯涵,满洲正黄旗人。曾任监国摄政王。

Qin Dechun (1893—1963) born in Yishui, Shandong, vice minister of national defense, and governor of Shandong Province during the republican era.

秦德纯(1893—1963),字绍文,山东沂水人。曾任国防部次长、山东省主席。

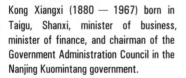

Kong Xiangxi (1880—1967) born in Taigu, Shanxi, minister of business, minister of finance, and chairman of the Government Administration Council in the Nanjing Kuomintang government.

孔祥熙(1880—1967),字庸之,山西太谷人。历任南京国民党政府实业部长、财政部部长、行政院院长等职。

Panchen Thupten Chokyi Nyima (1883—1937), the Ninth Panchen Lama, recognized by Emperor Guangxu in 1892. In 1923, he was squeezed out by the Dalai Lama. This picture was taken in 1924 when the Panchen Lama was in Lanzhou.

班禅额尔德尼·曲吉尼玛(1883—1937),西藏塔布准巴人,藏族。1892年经光绪皇帝批准在扎什伦布寺举行座床礼,为九世班禅。1910年后遭受达赖十三世排斥,1923年被迫出走。此系1924年途经兰州时所摄。

Xu Shichang (1855 — 1939) a native of Tianjin. War minister in the late Qing Dynasty and a president of the Republic of China.

徐世昌(1855—1939), 字卜五, 天津人。历任军机大臣、民国大总统。

Yan Huiqing (1877 — 1950) born in Shanghai. Foreign minister and minister of internal affairs in the Northern Warlords government. He went to Britain as ambassador of the Nanjing National government.

Song Zheyuan (1885 — 1940) born in Laoling, Shandong. Governor of Hebei Province, and a member of the Central Control Commission (of the CPC). During the Marco Polo Bridge Incident (July 7, 1937) he bravely led his army to fight against the Japanese invaders.

宋哲元(1885—1940), 字明轩, 山东乐陵人。曾任河北省政府主席。中央监察委员。1933年曾率部参加长城抗战,1937年"七·七事变"时,率部奋起抗战。

Jiang Chaozong (1864 — 1943) born in Jingde, Anhui. Puppet mayor of Peiping and a member of the Japanese-controlled North China Government Administrative Commission.

江朝宗(1864—1943), 字宇澄, 安徽旌德人。曾任满洲正黄旗都统、伪北平市长、伪华北政务委员会委员。

颜惠庆(1877—1950), 字骏人, 上海市人。历任北洋军阀政府外交部总长、内务部总长。国民南京政府成立后,任驻英大使。

Li Zongren (1891 — 1969) born in Guilin, Guangxi. Acting president of the Kuomintang Government.

李宗仁(1891—1969)，字德邻，广西桂林人。曾任国民党政府代总统。

Zai Zhen (1876 — 1948) Manchu. Minister of agriculture, industry and trade, Bideyuan Counselor during the late Qing Dynasty.

载振(1876—1948)，字育周，满洲镶蓝旗人。曾任农工商部尚书，清内阁弼德院顾问大臣。此照为载振及其夫人、小女等，在府弟绿意廊前的合影。

章宗祥(1879—1962)字仲和，浙江吴兴人。曾任驻日公使，司法总长。抗日期间，任伪华北政务委员会谘询委员。1919年任中国出席巴黎和会代表，"五四运动"中被斥为卖国贼而免职。图为1918年12月出席巴黎和会前夕与其夫人合影。

Zhang Zongxiang (1879 — 1962) born in Wuxing, Zhejiang. An envoy to Japan and a minister of justice. During the Anti-Japanese War, he was a consultant in the puppet North China Government Administrative Commission. In 1919, he attended the Paris Peace Conference as a Chinese representative. During the May Fourth Movement (1919) he was regarded as a traitor and removed from his office. Here is Zhang and his wife before the Pairs Peace Conference.

Wang Jingwei (1883 — 1944) born in Panyu, Guangdong.

汪精卫(1883—1944)，字秀新，名兆铭，生于广东番禺。原籍浙江绍兴。

Zhang Xueliang born Haicheng, Liaoning. Called the "Young Marshal", Zhang was the key figure in the Xi'an Incident of 1936, which brought about the United Front between the Kuomintang and the Communist Party on the eve of World War II in China.

张学良,字汉卿,辽宁海城人。此照摄于1928年6月。

Zhang Xueming (1907 — 1983) born in Haicheng, Liaoning. Mayor of Tianjin City during the republican era.

张学铭(1907—1983),辽宁海城人。民国时任天津市市长。

Chiang Kai-shek (1887 — 1975) born in Fenghua, Zhejiang.

蒋介石(1887—1975),又名中正,浙江奉化人。

图书在版编目 (CIP) 数据

旧中国掠影: 中英文对照/陈涌等编辑.
-北京: 中国画报出版社, 1996.6
ISBN 7-80024-297-8

I. 旧… II. 陈… III. 社会-概况-
中国-1869~1949-画册 IV. D693-64
中国版本图书馆CIP数据
核字 (96) 第08750号

旧中国掠影

名誉主任: 张家骅
编委主任: 黄祖安
编　委: 施庆华 李春生 陈月萍 赵春林
主　编: 陈　涌
总 策 划: 陈　涌
策　划: 赵春林
执行主编: 拓晓堂
责任编辑: 史维平 杨葵
审　校: SHAWN C.TRAYLOR
翻　译: 姜瀛
美术设计: 史维平
封面题字: 黄钟骏
本画册资料由中国画报社、北京图书馆
等单位提供

编　著: 中国画报社
　　　　新世纪之光编辑委员会
出　版: 中国画报出版社
印　制: 北京东方明珠文化发展公司
地　址: 中国北京海淀上地四街八号
邮政编码: 100085
电　话: 62983406—32
国外发行: 中国国际图书贸易总公司
地　址: 中国北京海淀区车公庄西路35号
信　箱: 北京邮政信箱第399号
邮政编码: 100044
开本大16开 印张 20张
图片 800张　文字 50千
1994年10月第1版 1994年10月第1次印刷
1996年 5月第2版 1996年 5月第2次印刷
版权所有　盗印必究
印数 3001—7000册
书号 ISBN7—80024—297—8/J•298
　　　　16000
　　　85—CE—476S

First Edition 1984
Second Edition 1995

A GLIMPSE OF OLD CHINA

Honorary Chairman: Zhang Jiahua
Chairman: Huang Zu'an
Members: Shi Qinghua Li Chunsheng
                    Chen Yueping Zhao Chunlin
Editor in Chief: Chen Yong
General Planning: Chen Yong
Planning: Zhao Chunlin
Executive Chief Editor: Tuo Xiaotang
English Translation: Shawn C. Traylor
                    Jiang Ying
Layout: Shi Weiping
Front Cover Inscription: Huang Zhongjun

Photographs in This Album are Provided by
the China Pictorial Publications and Beijing
National Library.

Edited By China Pictorial and the Editorial Board
of the Light of the New Century
Produced By
Beijing Dongfang Mingzhu Cultural Co., Ltd.
8, The Fourth Street, Shangdi, Haidian District,
Beijing 100085, China.
Phone for Order: 62983406—32
All Rights Reserved.
Distributed by
China International Book Trading Corporation
 35 Chegongzhuang Xilu, Beijing 100044, China
P.O. Box. 399, Beijing, China.

Printed in the People's Republic of China